Memos to the President

Memos to the President

Management Advice
from the Nation's
Top CEOs

EDITED WITH
AN INTRODUCTION BY
JAMES J. SCHIRO, CEO
PRICEWATERHOUSECOOPERS

John Wiley & Sons, Inc.

New York · Chichester · Weinheim · Brisbane · Singapore · Toronto

Contents

Acknowledgments   ix

Introduction   xi

I CREATING VISION

James P. Kelly   3
Chairman and Chief Executive Officer,
 United Parcel Service (UPS)
Communicating Your Vision—Creating a Charter
 for Your Administration

Edward J. Ludwig   11
President and Chief Executive Officer, BD
Getting Started—Creating a Distinct Vision

Sy Sternberg   21
Chairman, President, and Chief Executive Officer,
 New York Life Insurance Company
Making Important Decisions about Your Core Mission

Leonard D. Schaeffer   31
Chairman and Chief Executive Officer,
 WellPoint Health Networks Inc.
The Challenge of Leadership versus Management

Joseph Neubauer   37
Chairman and Chief Executive Officer,
    ARAMARK
Building Your Team and Setting a Vision

2   **MANAGING CHANGE**

James J. Schiro   47
Chief Executive Officer, PricewaterhouseCoopers
Managing Change

William R. Johnson   59
Chairman, President, and Chief Executive Officer,
    H. J. Heinz Company
Leadership for a Changing World

William D. Zollars   69
Chairman of the Board, President, and Chief
    Executive Officer, Yellow Corporation
Deploying Technology and Changing Culture

Edward A. Blechschmidt   81
Chairman, Chief Executive Officer, and President,
    Gentiva Health Services
Leading Change to Fulfill Your Strategic Vision

Eric Kuhn   89
President, Chief Executive Officer, and Cofounder,
    Varsity Group Inc.
The Importance of Knowing and Understanding
    Your Customers

3   **LEADING PEOPLE**

J. W. Marriott, Jr.   103
Chairman of the Board and Chief Executive Officer,
    Marriott International, Inc.
The Importance of People

Arthur M. Blank III
President and Chief Executive Officer,
The Home Depot
Managing in a Values-Driven Environment

Sidney Taurel II9
Chairman of the Board, President, and
Chief Executive Officer, Eli Lilly and Company
Leading People in Large Organizations

Archie W. Dunham 129
Chairman, President, and Chief Executive Officer,
Conoco Inc.
Sustaining a Learning Culture

Charles M. Brewer 137
Founder, MindSpring Enterprises, Inc.,
and Chairman, EarthLink, Inc.
Leading with Values

Fred Hassan 149
President and Chief Executive Officer,
Pharmacia Corporation
Changing Results by Changing Behaviors

Joseph D. Sargent 161
President and Chief Executive Officer, The Guardian
Life Insurance Company of America
Promoting Ethical Behavior
in Large Organizations

4 LEVERAGING TECHNOLOGY

Esther Dyson 171
Chairman, EDventure Holdings Inc.
Internet Privacy and Security Issues
You Face

Solomon D. Trujillo   181
Former Chairman, President, and
    Chief Executive Officer, U S WEST
Managing Technology and People
    in Large Organizations

Lars Nyberg   193
Chairman and Chief Executive Officer,
    NCR Corporation
Relationship Technologies: Managing
    in the Networked World

Earnest W. Deavenport, Jr.   203
Chairman and Chief Executive Officer,
    Eastman Chemical Company
Leveraging Information Technology

James J. Forese   211
Chairman and Chief Executive Officer,
    IKON Office Solutions
A Five-Step Plan for Improving Organizations

Richard Johnson   221
Founder, Chairman, Chief Executive Officer,
    and President, HotJobs.com
Technology and the New Economy

Appendix   227

Acknowledgments

As any editor knows, putting together a book is a major undertaking. There are many people whom I would like to thank and acknowledge for their participation in this project.

First, there are the chief executive officers who took time out of their busy schedules to write a memo for this project. As a CEO, I know the many demands on our time. I very much appreciate the time and effort put into this project by the participating CEOs.

Second, each of the CEOs participating in this book assigned one or two individuals in their corporation to serve as the liaison for the project. They were very helpful and served a key role in making the project a success. I would like to thank the following: Christopher Hardwick (ARAMARK), Camilla Jenkins (BD), Tom DeCola (Conoco), Colleen Dunn (EarthLink, Inc.), Tracy Bledsoe (Eastman Chemical), Terry Busch (Eli Lilly), Kimberly Herman and Jerry Mikorenda (Gentiva), Edward Selover (The Guardian Life Insurance Company of America), Jack Kennedy (H.J. Heinz), David Henry (The Home Depot), Jeannie Kim and Fianna Sogomony (HotJobs.com), Wendy Pickney and Steve Eck (IKON Office

Solutions), Nick Hill (Marriott International), Shelley Bird and Frank Ranew (NCR), Mike Mandato and Albert Johnston (New York Life Insurance), Ken Banta and Desiree Malanga (Pharmacia Corporation), Andrea Ziolkowski (US WEST), Steve Soltis (United Parcel Service), Jodi Gershon and Sam Heitner (Varsity Group Inc.), Carl Volpe (WellPoint Health Networks), and Roger Dick (Yellow).

Third, there was the PricewaterhouseCoopers oversight team for the project: Tom Craren, Bill Dauphinais, Joel Kurtzman, Roger Lipsey, and Bill Warren. All devoted their time and energies to making sure that the project was a success. Also lending key assistance in the project from PricewaterhouseCoopers were Vicky Palmer, Leslie Knauer, and Mark Misercola.

Fourth, every book needs a senior editor. We were blessed with an excellent one—Airié Dekidjiev from John Wiley & Sons. Airié constantly went above and beyond the call of duty in overseeing the development and production of this book.

Finally, I want to thank The PricewaterhouseCoopers Endowment for The Business of Government for their role in initiating and overseeing this project. Paul Lawrence, a partner at PricewaterhouseCoopers and cochair of The Endowment's Advisory Board brought the concept of the book to my attention last year and recommended that we undertake this project. Once it was launched, Paul kept a steady eye on the project and served on the PricewaterhouseCoopers oversight team. Mark Abramson, executive director of The Endowment, served as project director for the book. He managed the project from development to completion and worked closely with each of the company liaisons listed above. I appreciated his diligence and persistence throughout the project.

James J. Schiro

Introduction

James J. Schiro

Every new president enjoys an abundance of policy advice. Management advice is less plentiful. Yet the task of *managing* the federal government—including close to two million employees who work in the numerous departments and agencies that comprise the executive branch of government—is one of the president's most important responsibilities. In this day and age, leaders in all organizations—from the private-sector chief executive officers (CEOs) who have prepared the memos contained herein to leaders in the government and nonprofit sectors—must focus on the hard job of managing. The duties of today's manager include building a foundation, creating an inspiring vision, effectively communicating with employees, creating alliances during crucial times of change, hiring people who share your company's values, and harnessing the power of technology.

Memos to the President is based on a simple premise: The management challenges facing government, business, and the nonprofit sectors today are more similar than they are different. The CEOs who participated in this project believe that the insights they have gained in managing large organizations are transferrable to other organizations. Executives in all three sectors face enormous challenges in leading and managing their organizations. The goal of this book is to share the experiences of some of the nation's best CEOs with both the president-elect of the United States and the men and women who run departments and agencies and conduct the business of government. The information in this book will also be invaluable to managers in all sectors—public, private, and nonprofit.

Memos to the President is also based on the premise that managing in the first decade of the twenty-first century will be dramatically different. In the not-too-distant "old days," executives could set out on a course of action and expect to stick to that game plan for many years. The CEO could even take the people in his or her organization for granted, knowing they would likely be there for the remainder of their careers. Neither assumption is valid in today's business environment. Executives must now be nimble and agile and constantly look to adjust course when needed. In my memo, I discuss how PricewaterhouseCoopers has basically reinvented itself twice in the last two years to respond to a changing environment. As for our employees, we no longer assume that they will be with us for their entire careers—we must constantly work hard to recruit new employees and retain present employees in an increasingly competitive environment.

When we set out on this project in 1999, we wrote to CEOs all over the country, and in many fields, asking them if they wanted to participate. We did not specify which topics they should address in their memo. Instead, we let them determine which management issues would be most important for the president-elect of the United States to consider. In the end, we were surprised at the convergence of ideas. We found the key issues selected by our participating CEOs clustered around four very important executive responsibilities:

1. Creating an inspiring and consistent vision.
2. Managing change within the organization and preparing for external change.
3. Recruiting, retaining, and developing employees.
4. Leveraging technology to improve internal operations and the delivery of services to customers.

The more-than-20 CEOs who participated in this project draw on their own valuable experiences and share the insights they have gained in managing large organizations to address these issues. Their specific case examples and advice will be invaluable to public, private, and nonprofit sector leaders and also we hope to the new president and his appointed executives.

The President as Executive in Chief

While the president's role as commander in chief has long attracted the public's and the media's attention, the increased importance of his role as "executive in chief" has attracted scant notice. In today's world, the public has come to expect first-class customer service and performance from both business and government. Each day, Americans undertake a variety of activities in their daily routines. They purchase products either in a store, over the phone, or over the Internet. They make travel and dinner reservations. They use an automatic teller machine or conduct banking transactions over the phone or on-line. They also call government offices to ask questions, ranging from an inquiry about their mother's Medicare claim to requesting a social security number for a new child. In all these encounters, they expect a speedy, reliable, and courteous response. They have come to expect the same quality of service from both business and government. The challenge facing the next president will be to make sure that government can deliver the high quality of service that citizens have come to expect.

Government performance is not limited to satisfying the need to provide better customer service. The president and the federal government today have enormous responsibilities—ranging from safeguarding our national security at the Department of Defense to safeguarding the quality of our air and water at the Environmental Protection Agency. The federal government is also engaged in undertaking research and development in areas such as health (National Institutes of Health), transportation (Department of Transportation), and agriculture (Agriculture Research Service). In all these instances, the government performs its responsibilities through the people working in its many organizations. To fully accomplish its mission, both the individuals working in organizations and the organization as a whole have to perform to their maximum capability. The CEOs included in this book argue that that challenge is no different in the private sector than it is in the public sector. Running any organization—of any size in any sector—is a major challenge.

New Ideas

In reading through the memos in this book, you will be impressed by the many good ideas contributed by each of the participating CEOs. We believe that managers in all sectors can all learn from the actual practices of these outstanding leaders. Specifically, our CEOs present ideas such as the following:

- James P. Kelly, chairman and CEO of United Parcel Service (UPS), discusses the concept of creating *charters* for organizations, which include not only the organization's values but also its purpose, mission, and strategy.
- Joseph Neubauer, chairman and CEO of ARAMARK, recommends that organizations, such as federal departments and agencies, create "war-on-talent" *councils* to manage their recruitment initiatives.
- Ed Ludwig, president and CEO of Becton Dickinson, describes how he hosts a *CEO call-in* in which he takes phone calls from his employees to discuss critical issues in health care and to hear them describe their experiences on the front lines.
- Arthur Blank, president and CEO of The Home Depot, describes how he and all members of his board of directors go on *site visits* to a certain number of stores each quarter to talk directly with Home Depot associates and hear firsthand their suggestions and assessments of how the organization is currently running.

Creating Vision and Managing Change

While vision and change are often repeated in the mantra of good management practices, they have taken on added importance today because of the increased rapidity of change in all sectors. Hardly a day goes by without a new merger or megamerger in the headlines. Many of the CEOs in this book have undergone such change in their own organizations. Turbulence in the environment makes it even more important to (1) set forth an exciting vision that will both inspire and mobilize employees and the larger community and (2) manage the organizational change process in which a company or agency leaves behind its former self and becomes something new.

Creating the Vision. James P. Kelly, chairman and CEO of UPS describes how UPS created a charter for itself that established "a bridge between our fundamental values and the daily decisions of thousands of UPS managers. It provides meaning and coherence for our people as they do their work. Most important of all, it charts a clear course in the face of many competing forces." Other CEOs echo the importance of having a clear vision.

Leonard Schaeffer, chairman and CEO of WellPoint Health Networks, Inc., writes that vision is one of the most important aspects of a president's symbolic leadership. He recommends that the next president define and communicate his vision and provide "a clear picture of the future" for his administration, the American public, and the world.

Communicating the Vision. In the words of Edward J. Ludwig, president and CEO of Becton Dickinson and Company, "The pursuit of good communication is a never-ending journey." Ludwig writes that CEOs must "communicate, communicate, communicate." To improve communications, Ludwig regularly sends out memos—directly from him—to all employees to keep them apprised of significant business activities and decisions. "By communicating the context for decisions being made to the company at large, you foster a sense of ownership and involvement on everyone's part," writes Ludwig.

Reevaluating Core Missions. Many of the CEOs in this book describe a key task of the organizational leader—leading an assessment of the organization's mission. Is it in the right businesses? This becomes extremely important in government when missions accumulate over the years and a "house cleaning" may be needed. But such an organizational assessment should not automatically lead to the conclusion that everything needs to change. Sy Sternberg, chairman, president, and CEO of New York Life Insurance Company, describes the process of how New York Life reevaluated its core mission and decided *not* to follow the herd and the conventional wisdom. After considering its options, New York Life decided to stay in the life insurance business, not offer additional financial services, to continue with its successful agency system, and retain its basic structure. Sternberg writes, "A corporate culture isn't something you *have*, it's what you *are*. You can become better, more effective, more efficient without becoming something else."

Bringing about Change. But sometimes change is imperative. The key is making the right change in the right way. A poorly implemented change initiative often leaves an organization even further behind than it would have been had it opted for the status quo. In his memo, William Johnson, president and CEO of H.J. Heinz, reflects on the Heinz change experience and recommends that change must be quick and pervasive, highly relevant, and personal to succeed in any organization. Johnson writes, "Change is at work everywhere, constantly redefining our environment and our constituencies. . . . In such an environment, a leader who wishes to take command of change must act quickly and operate across a broad field. Hesitant, incremental actions are easily overwhelmed. Bold, broad initiatives alone can move an organization forward."

You should not, however, underestimate the magnitude of the change task. William D. Zollars, chairman, president, and CEO of Yellow Corporation, describes how changing an existing organization is one of the hardest things that a company or agency can do. He likens it to changing a company's DNA and concludes that it cannot be done in a month or two because it requires "constant and relentless attack over a long period of time."

Successfully Implementing Change. Although change is difficult, there are key actions that organizational leaders can take to improve the process. Edward Blechschmidt, chairman, CEO, and president of Gentiva Health Services, describes the key factors that enabled Gentiva to change for the better, including effective and honest communication, rewards and recognition, speed, and active risk management. "Managed properly," writes Blechschmidt, "change can lead to renewed focus and passion, new processes, realignment of resources, and organizational efficiency."

After initiating the change process, executives must constantly keep an eye on the changing environment and be able to respond quickly to new changes. Eric Kuhn, president, CEO, and cofounder of Varsity Group, Inc., describes the key characteristics that have allowed his organization to respond to his environment and constituents: remain agile, maximize resources, and maintain vision. But every leader must also constantly remember his or her strategic vision. "The importance of remaining swift and nimble is not . . . eclipsed by the continued importance to remain strategic," cautions Kuhn. "Our quick strike efforts made possible by our agility are always guided by an overall strategic plan."

Leading People

Frankly, I was pleasantly surprised that our contributors share my view that among the most important tasks of any chief executive are leading people, devoting time to recruitment and retention issues, and overseeing the implementation of world-class executive development activities. J.W. Marriott, chairman and CEO of Marriott International, writes, "Finding the right people to meet the demands of our organization is always a challenge, but perhaps never more so than today."

This is an area, conclude several of the CEOs, in which the government is ripe for change. In his memo, Sidney Taurel, chairman, president and CEO of Eli Lilly and Company, writes to the president-elect: "This 'people' avenue is neither obvious nor glamorous, to be sure, and it is filled with formidable obstacles. . . . To make your mark as a true leader and a great manager, I would urge you to press for dramatic reform of, first, the rules and, ultimately the culture of the federal civil service."

The Importance of Ethics and Values. Several of our participating CEOs discussed ethics. Joseph Sargent, CEO of the Guardian Life Insurance Company of America, describes the 140-year history of Guardian Life and how it has fostered high ethical behavior over that time period by creating a culture that communicates "we do the right thing." Sargent writes, "The right way ultimately proves the best way, whether in business or public affairs."

In his memo, Arthur M. Blank, president and CEO of The Home Depot, discusses the importance of selecting individuals to high positions who share your values. "Finding the right people for the most important jobs means, first and foremost, attracting those who share the same basic values upon which you base your heartfelt and momentous decisions," writes Blank.

Charles M. Brewer, founder of MindSpring Enterprises, Inc., and chairman of EarthLink, Inc., describes the importance of core values and beliefs to his entire organization. Brewer recalls, "When I set out to start a company in the spring of 1993, I didn't know what the company would do, but I had some very firm ideas about what the culture would be like—how we would treat each other, and how we would treat our customers." Brewer also emphasizes the importance of using the "metrics, systems, and processes" of an organization to support the organization's core values and not work against them.

People as a Key Resource. Leading people, argue our CEOs, is based on the premise that people are important and the key to organizational success. This view was clearly articulated by J.W. Marriott, Jr., who writes, "Whatever the situation, our success as an organization rests in large measure on one critical factor: our people." Marriott recalls what he learned from his father about leading people, who told him, "Take care of your employees, and they'll take care of your customers." He describes Marriott's programs to create a supportive environment for all employees.

Closely linked to the concept of using people as a resource is the idea of fostering an environment in which the "right behaviors" are encouraged. Fred Hassan, president and CEO of Pharmacia Corporation, writes, "The kinds of behaviors that we are demanding of our managers are not easy to instill, because many of them run counter to territorial human instincts. So we've also devoted great time and effort to rewarding the right behaviors among managers—assuring, in other words, what we *say* in this critical area is what our people also *do*." In striving to become the "best-managed" company in their industry, Pharmacia selected five "best-managed" behaviors, which include participative management, continuous improvement, listening and learning, and coaching. Hassan argues that participative management has had a direct positive impact on the company—speeding up the company's ability to move from discovery of a new medicine to regulatory approval in rapid time.

Selecting People. Another theme is the importance of attracting and selecting talent, especially in this era of the "war for talent." Joseph Neubauer, chairman and CEO of ARAMARK, notes that he is personally involved in hiring the top 75 people in his company. Like many of the CEOs in this book, he has learned some key lessons about the hiring process: You must be personally involved in the interviewing process, you must seek people who have different and diverse backgrounds, you must be willing to take a chance on people, and you must work to depoliticize the process.

Sol Trujillo, former chairman, president, and CEO of U S WEST, emphasizes the importance of promoting diversity. Trujillo writes, "Minorities now constitute nearly 30 percent of the U.S. population, and that percentage will continue to grow. These numbers alone have transformed diversity from 'nice to do' to 'must do' as organizations scramble to find qualified workers and market to an increasing diverse U.S. population. But if the numbers aren't enough to convince an organization of the value of fostering diversity, its benefits—a more dynamic, productive employee body more capable of responding to the needs of customers—surely will."

Developing People. Several CEOs describe the importance of developing their personnel. Sidney Taurel explains that Eli Lilly and Company has established employee development as management's number-one priority. "We make a deep and systematic commitment," writes Taurel, "to ensure that our people continually acquire, extend, and renew the skills they need not just to maintain but actually grow their value to the organization."

Archie W. Dunham, chairman, president, and CEO of Conoco, Inc., describes Conoco's Trailblazer program, which is aimed at training future leaders who, over time, will create a new management model for Conoco. Dunham believes that investing in the development of people will be a defining factor in the success of organizations in the future. "Attracting and retaining outstanding people and challenging them to develop to their full potential is a critical necessity of both industry and government," writes Dunham.

Leveraging Technology

The fourth common theme is leveraging technology. As individuals who have witnessed firsthand the impact of technology in substantially improving their own organizations, these CEOs have become champions for all organizations to use technology to improve customer service and internal operations. Sol Trujillo sums this up well: "The Information Age has just begun, and with it comes an opportunity for both business and government to realize unprecedented gains in productivity."

Earnest Deavenport, Jr., chairman and CEO of Eastman Chemical Company, describes how a basic manufacturing company like Eastman Chemical transformed itself in this digital age. "It's simple," writes Deavenport. "We move from a 'bricks-and-mortar' company, to a 'clicks-and-mortar' company. If an old-line chemical company can leverage technology, the potential for the federal government to leverage technology is equally great, if not greater."

Leveraging technology, however, will require financial investments. William Zollars of Yellow Corporation described his "2-to-1 Rule." "For every dollar invested in legacy system support, we invest two dollars in development of new systems and technology," writes Zollars. "In addition to employing the '2-to-1 Rule,' we avoid programs and projects that take more than three years to complete. The entire industry has moved on by the time those projects are finished."

Managing the Net. A major management challenge facing the next president will be his role in "managing the net" and responding to issues related to privacy and security. In her memo, Esther Dyson, chairman of EDventure Holdings, advises: "Most of what you should do vis-à-vis the Net is to show restraint. . . . All you need to do is avoid imposing too much control (Do not attempt to regulate content! Let parents monitor their kids!), while at the same time fostering a Net that is robust and secure."

Unleashing the Potential of E-Commerce. Several CEOs commented on the enormous potential of e-commerce on government. Sol Trujillo writes, "Stepping up e-commerce is essential to the success of any large organization in the new economy. Doing things electronically can increase productivity while reducing costs, two things that were often mutually exclusive in the pre-e-commerce world." Trujuillo also provides advice to organizations making the transition to e-commerce: start at the top, invest in infrastructure, appoint the right people to key jobs, and insist on e-commerce in procurement.

Implications of the Networked World. In his memo, Lars Nyberg, chairman and CEO of NCR Corporation, discusses the new networked world in which "traditional barriers to productivity and interactions, such as time and distance, are eliminated." "The network is perpetually 'on,' connecting people and devices seamlessly," writes Nyberg. He argues that all organizations, including government, must begin to respond to the demand for increased customer service. Nyberg recommends the use of relationship technologies to build stronger bonds with customers.

Building Business-to-Business Solutions. A major theme of several of the memos is the potential of improving the internal operations of organizations through the use of technology. Earnest Deavenport describes how business-to-business solutions have changed his organization. "As in any company, it is critical that we receive quality goods and services from our suppliers in a timely and simplified manner," writes Deavenport. "Technology has allowed us to provide Web-based procurement, which means that our employees now have on-line access to suppliers' catalogs for direct ordering of materials."

Implementing Technology Solutions. James J. Forese, president and CEO of IKON Office Solutions, cautions that implementing the latest digital technologies will yield little if it simply automates obsolete or obsolescent processes. Forese recommends that organizations identify processes that need to be revised, replaced, or simply eliminated. The identification process should take place through a comprehensive examination of how work flows throughout an organization. Forese writes, "The key word there is 'comprehensive.' It is not cost-effective to approach systems upgrades in a gradual way, adding a new component here or there."

The Challenge Ahead

Americans have always embraced change and looked to the future with great optimism. The next four years should be truly a revolutionary time in government and business. The first decade of the new century should be a particularly exciting period for leaders in all sectors—public, private, and nonprofit. It is truly an exciting new ball game for executives everywhere.

Today, at the dawn of the twenty-first century, we welcome a new president, a new administration, and the promise of a fresh beginning. Our shared faith in the United States' capacity for rebirth and renewal accounts for the enthusiasm with which our contributors have shared their experiences, thoughts, and advice. Like all Americans, we want the new president to succeed.

I hope that this volume will be of value to executives everywhere, as the new president and his administration grapple with the enormous managerial tasks ahead. We can all take heart from the fact that—like the CEOs who've written memos for this book—executives today have more tools (electronic and otherwise) at their disposal than did any of their predecessors. As CEOs, we have seen a revolution in private-sector management. The time may now be ripe for such a revolution in the public sector. The new president can take what the private sector has done, as well as what many organizations in the public and nonprofit sectors have done, and build on these endeavors to create something unique—a federal government redesigned for the demands of a digital age. A notable legacy indeed.

1

CREATING
VISION

JAMES P. KELLY

James P. Kelly is chairman and chief executive officer of UPS, elected in 1997. He joined UPS in 1964 as a package car driver and entered supervision two years later. He became U.S. Operations Manager in 1990. In 1992 he became chief operating officer and was appointed executive vice president in 1994. Mr. Kelly holds a bachelor of science degree in management from Rutgers University.

James P. Kelly
Chairman, Chief Executive Officer

MEMORANDUM

TO: President-elect of the United States

FROM: James P. Kelly, Chairman and Chief Executive
Officer, United Parcel Service (UPS)

SUBJECT: Communicating Your Vision—
Creating a Charter for Your Administration

In the time of transition from candidacy to presidency, I imagine you'll begin to feel the weight of the personal challenge you
will bear every day throughout your term. That challenge is to
translate your vision of America's future into action through the
federal government.

I'm sure you've already reflected on those of your predecessors who took office with great promise but left no enduring
legacy. Some were overtaken by unforeseen events; others
simply lacked a sufficiently detailed plan for harnessing the
powers of government from the beginning. Your record as
president will be written in the hundreds of decisions large
and small made under your leadership from the first day of
your term to the last. In order to ensure that those decisions
are aligned with your aspirations for the country, you and your
executive team will need a clearly articulated plan.

Therefore, I urge you at this early date to create a written framework—a charter—to guide everyone in your administration toward the goals you want to achieve as president. In my view, such a charter will be indispensable as you face the tough job of imprinting the ideas and intentions of your election campaign on the daily agendas of people throughout the executive branch.

The document I have in mind, formulated prior to the start of your tenure with the help of trusted advisors, should state in clear, direct language how your administration will go about the task of governing the United States. It will signal your intentions to three important audiences: your appointees, your federal workforce, and the American people. By articulating your plan for governing prior to taking the oath of office, you stand to gain early momentum.

I URGE YOU AT THIS EARLY DATE TO CREATE A WRITTEN FRAMEWORK—A CHARTER—TO GUIDE EVERYONE IN YOUR ADMINISTRATION TOWARD THE GOALS YOU WANT TO ACHIEVE AS PRESIDENT.

There will be those who question the need for the kind of separate, specific document described in this memo. They will argue that the Declaration of Independence and Constitution provide all the "vision and mission" you or any other president require. However, there is a substantial distance between the awesome principles expressed in those bedrock documents and the thousands of federal policies, regulatory rules, and laws that will be enacted during your term. I believe you need a charter for your administration to ensure that each small decision is consistent with our national ideals.

THE [CHARTER] SHOULD STATE IN CLEAR, DIRECT LANGUAGE HOW YOUR ADMINISTRATION WILL GO ABOUT . . . GOVERNING THE UNITED STATES. IT WILL SIGNAL YOUR INTENTIONS TO THREE IMPORTANT AUDIENCES: YOUR APPOINTEES, YOUR FEDERAL WORKFORCE, AND THE AMERICAN PEOPLE.

The U.S. government has much in common with other large organizations whose success depends on the link between collective values and individual decisions. At United Parcel Service, our 330,000 employees operate an incredibly complex worldwide enterprise. On a daily basis they execute our corporate strategies, which are constantly adjusting to new realities. The actions of each person, from driver to chairman, have a tangible impact on the performance of the entire company. Our goal is consistent, competitive performance.

For 92 years, strong leadership and insightful guidance ensured that our objectives were well understood and well executed throughout the company. But the world is evolving more rapidly now. Change comes by the hour, the minute, even the second. Decisions being made around the clock and around the world by UPSers in this era of global e-commerce are usually in response to immediate local issues. Without a detailed plan to instill our guiding principles in each of those decisions, we risk a creeping myopia that can eventually bring down the performance of the most durable organization.

I BELIEVE YOU NEED A CHARTER FOR YOUR ADMINISTRATION TO ENSURE THAT EACH SMALL DECISION IS CONSISTENT WITH OUR NATIONAL IDEALS.

Last year the leaders of our company created a new kind of document we call the UPS Charter. It creates a bridge between our fundamental values and the daily decisions of thousands of UPS managers. It provides meaning and coherence for our people as they do their work. Most important of all, it charts a clear course in the face of many competing forces.

Defining Values, Purpose, Mission, and Strategy

The architecture of the UPS Charter is a series of concentric circles. In the center, at the heart of our organization, are our company's values. In the face of rapidly changing conditions, these values remain steadfast. They are our enduring beliefs, informing and guiding everything and everyone in the organization.

Wrapped around our values is our purpose as an organization. Perhaps the single most important phrase in the UPS

Charter is "enabling global commerce." The wording couldn't be more simple or clear—or more profound for our business. It is also steadfast; because of our unique history and strategic decisions over the past two decades, UPS now spans all three flows of commerce: goods, information, and funds.

In the next circle is our mission—what we seek to achieve as we live out the values and purpose of UPS. The outermost circle of the UPS Charter is our strategy: our current plan of action. This strategy is not etched in stone. It must remain highly dynamic to address changes in our business environment. Never again will our strategy be a single statement or idea that fits neatly in a frame or on a pocket card.

Anticipating Change

One of my predecessors as chairman of UPS, George Smith, provided some wisdom in this area more than 40 years ago. "Each day conditions change, our nation changes, the business world changes, the needs of our customers change," he said. "As we learn more, . . . our ideas change, our goals and objectives change. So we, as an organization, are constantly changing, living, and growing."

The UPS Charter is designed to accommodate change, so it is not a static statement on paper but a living, breathing document. By embedding change in the business plans of all our functional areas, we not only reinforce the charter but also ensure that it will be regularly updated in the context of the realities of our business.

We actively promote the concepts in our charter at every opportunity, because, like the U.S. government, our organization is widely dispersed and it requires extra effort to keep messages flowing in both directions. We revisit our charter at our annual managers' conference and disseminate it to all our people through both informal and formal means. You can "hear" the principles in our charter at work at the daily two-minute Prework Communication Meetings that involve every employee in the company, in our press releases, our marketing literature and direct mailings, even in the speeches our executives deliver at major conferences.

The Charter in Action

Has our charter helped UPS achieve our goals? It certainly has. In the brief time since we enacted the charter in 1999, our company made a highly successful first public offering, entered new markets around the world, and added innovative new services to the industry's broadest portfolio of offerings. We continued to invest in advancing technologies and expanded our expertise in supply-chain management. And we accomplished all that while fulfilling historic commitments to our employees, our communities, and our shareholders.

The UPS Charter is not intended to define every opportunity on the horizon or predict every outcome of our actions and strategies. But it does articulate our current leaders' vision for moving the company forward. It provides the simple, tangible statements that anchor the efforts of all of us at UPS.

In fulfilling our charter, we retain the best of what UPS is—our sense of who we are and what we stand for—as we meet many new challenges. I believe a similar charter would serve as a valuable guide to make your new administration as effective as you now hope it will be. I would encourage you to ask each member of your cabinet to prepare a charter for their respective departments.

As you anticipate your first day as president, let me ask you to pause and think of your last day in office. As you await your successor at the front portico of the White House, how satisfied will you be with the achievements of your administration? Will you feel that your vision for America's future was adequately realized? I sincerely hope so, and for that reason I urge you to call together the close group of people who share your vision to draft a charter that will ensure a lasting legacy for your administration and a brighter future for all Americans.

EDWARD J. LUDWIG

Edward J. Ludwig is president and chief executive officer of BD (Becton, Dickinson and Company). Mr. Ludwig joined BD in 1979 and worked in various management positions, becoming senior vice president and chief financial officer in 1995. Previously, Mr. Ludwig was with Coopers and Lybrand and with Walter Kidde, Inc. Mr. Ludwig earned his bachelor of arts degree in economics and accounting at Holy Cross College and his master of business administration degree in finance from Columbia University.

1 Becton Drive
Franklin Lakes, New Jersey 07417
tel: 201.847.6800
www.bd.com

**Indispensable to
human health**

MEMORANDUM

TO: President-elect of the United States
FROM: Edward J. Ludwig, President and Chief Executive
           Officer, BD (Becton, Dickinson and Company)
SUBJECT: Getting Started—Creating a Distinct Vision

For the past nine months I have served as the president and
chief executive officer of BD (Becton, Dickinson and Company),
where I have worked for the past 21 years. BD is a 103-year-old
medical technology firm that manufactures and sells a broad
range of medical devices and diagnostic systems. We are headquartered in New Jersey, but our 23,000 employees serve health
care customers from more than 80 BD operational bases around
the world.

  You may think it brash for a novice CEO to be offering
advice to the next president of the United States—I know I do!
But despite the obvious differences between us in terms of the
size of the enterprises we serve and the leadership challenges
we face, I believe some of what I have learned in my early days
as CEO may be useful. As one new CEO to another, I would
like to share with you my experiences over the past year.

Assess the Overall Strategic Direction of Your Enterprise

A new leader has a brief period of time in which to reevaluate the enterprise and adjust or revise the course as he or she sees fit. In my case, as a longtime member of BD's senior management team, I had participated in setting the strategy for our company for a number of years before being named CEO. This history made for a smoother transition when I became CEO, but even so, I took advantage of my "honeymoon period" to revisit the corporation's overall strategy and direction.

Engage and Involve Others in the Organization in Setting Your Strategic Direction

In revisiting the BD corporate strategy, I met and talked at length with the BD Leadership Team—our company's cabinet, if you will—which is made up of senior business leaders and corporate function heads. To supplement our understanding of how well the entire organization understood our strategy, designated BD leaders held "town meetings" (we call them "profile sessions") with small groups of employees to see how they perceived the clarity of our direction and focus. We held dozens of these sessions and heard from literally thousands of our employees from around the world. Representatives from each of these sessions presented their findings and insights to the Leadership Team during the first month of my tenure as CEO. Out of this exchange of information came a recommitment to our purpose as a company: *to help all people live healthy lives.* We also learned that there was a greater need for clarity around *how* we were going to achieve this noble aspiration. There was a call for a greater investment in training and development of our employees and a need to streamline many important business processes.

Our discussions in those early days were invaluable in helping to make sure that all BD employees understood our purpose and strategy and could therefore work together with our leadership to support them. We were able to gain consensus around the purpose and strategy very effectively because of the in-depth involvement and participation of so many people.

In all of these discussions I tried hard to listen and learn from our strong Leadership Team. An invaluable by-product of this team process was that I had an early opportunity to meet with and engage BD leaders very directly and show them my commitment to helping others solve problems—at the same time acknowledging their critical roles in the company's future.

Make Your Own Mark Early On

Because I'd been with BD for many years, I'd already had ample time to learn about our history and to absorb the BD culture—and even to help shape them in some ways. Still, it was critical for me to put my own stamp and personality as a CEO on the company right away. We had recommitted to our purpose and corporate strategy and, although it was not a huge shift in course, it gave us a sharpened focus on how we hope to grow and develop looking forward.

The next step for me was to put my leadership mark on the way we chose to articulate our identity and our aspirations as a company. Within the first weeks of my tenure as CEO, I sent a memo to all BD employees defining the three critical areas in which we would strive for excellence:

- We strive to make a great contribution to improving medical practice around the world.
- We are committed to achieving great performance results.
- We want to become a great place to work.

These are not totally new BD aspirations, but they do reflect the company's goals in a fresh way that capture the great challenges and opportunities of today, reflect the perspective of our Leadership Team, and carry my own personal stamp as a new CEO. Whether you plan to employ massive changes right away or to take small steps, you too will need to communicate from the beginning your perspective on a wide array of issues.

Recognize That You Are an Important Enabler of a Successful Enterprise—But Not Always the Doer

BD has 23,000 employees around the world, a fraction of the workforce you manage as head of the United States government, but no small number. I have no illusions about being the sole manager of this large a group. My role is to communicate clearly that every BD manager—beginning with the CEO—is an enabler, a coach, and a teacher. The people on the front line know best; a good leader should focus on helping people arrive at the right conclusions—and get out of their way when the time is right!

Demonstrate Your Commitment to Creating a Great Work Environment

The job market has never been tighter, but in any era getting and keeping the best talent is a critical challenge for every organization, public or private. Great companies are also great places to work, and greatness depends on people, how they work together and how they think. Several years ago, BD embarked on a transformation journey to create an environment that encourages individual initiative but also fosters collaboration across traditional business and geographic boundaries. When we reassessed BD's direction in my early days as CEO, it became clear that we had a long way to go before this transformed environment could become a reality. We moved quickly to develop and introduce a "BD University"—a worldwide virtual-learning system, offering tools and training to help BD employees develop and hone their leadership skills. The BD Human Resources organization is developing the curriculum and BD executives are serving as teachers and trainers. This year, a group of BD business leaders is piloting a course titled "Coaching for Performance and Development" to help leaders understand their role as coaches in creating a high-performance, empowering work environment.

WHETHER YOU PLAN TO EMPLOY MASSIVE CHANGES RIGHT AWAY OR TO TAKE SMALL STEPS, YOU TOO WILL NEED TO COMMUNICATE FROM THE BEGINNING YOUR PERSPECTIVE ON A WIDE ARRAY OF ISSUES.

Identify and Articulate Your Core Values

A few years ago, BD went through a lengthy process of corporate self-discovery aimed at identifying the values unique to our company and people. As president of the United States, you need look no further than the Declaration of Independence for the most inspiring words ever written to capture the essential values of our nation. The BD values had been lived out for many years but had never been articulated. To do so was imperative if we were to perpetuate our main precepts as we entered our second century.

We based the identification of our core values on the management insights of Jim Collins, a consultant and coauthor of the book *Built to Last*, which studies the successful habits of visionary companies in order to help other organizations strive for greater success. Collins inspired us to confirm the timeless qualities that set BD apart.

We conducted employee town meetings around the world to come to an agreement that our fundamental values, in a world of change and challenge, remain constant and unchanging. We printed cards for all employees that state the four core values that unite us in our work and in our actions:

- *we act in harmony;*
- *we do what is right;*
- *we always seek to improve; and*
- *we accept individual responsibility.*

The federal government has equally compelling values. Your Department of Health and Human Services also strives to help people lead healthy lives. It will be incumbent upon you and your cabinet secretaries to articulate these historical values and reinforce their importance to your employees so as to be responsive to the evolving needs of our citizens in this new century.

Communicate, Communicate, Communicate

The pursuit of good communications is a never-ending journey. For any complex organization, effective communication is both an individual obligation and an organizational challenge. I have made it my top priority to communicate openly and broadly throughout our far-reaching operations, and to insist that good communications practice be fundamental in all BD organizations and relationships—from worldwide businesses to small-project teams. As with all company objectives, leaders must set the example. One way I have tried to do this is by making sure that as many employees as possible receive regular memos—directly from me—that keep them apprised of significant business activities and decisions. By communicating the context for decisions being made to the company at large, you foster a sense of ownership and involvement on everyone's part.

THE PURSUIT OF GOOD COMMUNICATIONS IS A NEVER-ENDING JOURNEY. FOR ANY COMPLEX ORGANIZATION, EFFECTIVE COMMUNICATION IS BOTH AN INDIVIDUAL OBLIGATION AND AN ORGANIZATIONAL CHALLENGE.

Despite all the resources available in our high-tech age, we've opted for a wonderfully low-tech way to create a real sense of connection among BD people around the globe. Every quarter we have a "CEO call-in" (when I play radio talk-show host). All employees get the opportunity to call and ask me questions about just about anything. The response to this approach of direct communication in a nonthreatening forum has been terrific. (And sometimes the questions have been tough!) These methods empower employees to ask for and therefore enact change. Whenever a CEO can provide employees with direct access to senior management in a casual format, he or she should take the opportunity. It is a stimulating and humbling experience for me to listen to so many talented people discuss the critical issues we face in health care today and describe their experiences on the front lines. It is a learning experience that renews my motivation to be the best leader I can be.

The impact and importance of maintaining direct contact with the "real world" outside of the executive wing hit home for me recently when I attended the 50th anniversary of one of our manufacturing facilities, located in Columbus, Nebraska. As I stood greeting hundreds of current and retired employees, a retired couple approached and shook my hand. I did not know them. They told me they had begun working at the plant 50 years ago, before I was born. They had met, married, and raised a family in that community. The husband looked me in the eye and said, "Thank you. Everything we have—our meeting and marriage, our family and our home—we owe these to BD. Thank you." The encounter moves me to this day and I feel fortunate for every such reminder that it is the people who make a company great, not the CEO. I am glad I had the presence of mind to respond, "No, sir, you are not right. It is BD, as a company and as a community of 23,000 people, who is truly indebted to you and your wife. On behalf of them and the customers we serve, I thank you."

In closing, I want to sincerely wish you every success as the newest leader of our great nation. The early period of your tenure will be marked with importance and excitement. As you create your vision, put your own personal stamp on living the values embodied in our Constitution, determine your business practices, and focus on communicating effectively, you will be setting the foundation for a new government that is "built to last."

SY STERNBERG

S y Sternberg is chairman, president, and chief executive officer of New York Life Insurance Company, the nation's fourth largest life insurer. He has been president of the company since 1995. He previously served as senior executive vice president of the Massachusetts Mutual Life Insurance Company. Mr. Sternberg received a bachelor of science degree from the City College of New York and a master of science degree from Northeastern University.

New York Life Insurance Company
51 Madison Avenue, New York, NY 10010

Sy Sternberg, CLU
Chairman, President and
Chief Executive Officer

MEMORANDUM

TO: President-elect of the United States

FROM: Sy Sternberg, Chairman, President, and Chief Executive Officer, New York Life Insurance Company

SUBJECT: Making Important Decisions about Your Core Mission

The job of leading a government of 14 cabinet departments and numerous independent agencies poses tremendous challenges. Each of the men and women you appoint to run the many divisions of your organization will have one task in common: They'll have to make important decisions about where to focus their own energy and the resources of their organizations. New questions, problems, and issues will arrive constantly—based on a constant stream of information from members of Congress and committees, from the media, from business, labor, advocacy groups, and poll takers. The options for your executives will be numerous:

- Should I take on new missions?
- Should I pare back on existing ones?

- Should I develop new priorities?
- Should I focus only on the essential?

There will also be added pressure to trend-watch, to let the zeitgeist and conventional wisdom determine the course of action that you and your appointees take. It's understandable enough why many choose management directives in response to what others have chosen; the safest course often appears to be the popular one—there is less opposition and less chance of being second-guessed if the majority is on board.

In my experience at New York Life, I have found that the best course has often been to buck the trend, to look closely at your organization's core mission and let that—rather than the actions of your competitors—guide you. The simple secret is to know who you are and what you stand for, and act accordingly. There is nothing more important a chief executive officer can do to improve his organization than to lead it in reexamining itself and deciding what business it's in and how best to conduct that business.

> I HAVE FOUND THAT THE BEST COURSE HAS OFTEN BEEN TO BUCK THE TREND, TO LOOK CLOSELY AT YOUR ORGANIZATION'S CORE MISSION AND LET THAT . . . GUIDE YOU.

In working through this process, keep in mind that following conventional wisdom presents its own set of risks. There are times when the best chance of success is to adopt a contrarian point of view. Sometimes determining your own course may even mean staying right where you are despite the general bias toward action.

This viewpoint is not based on idle speculation. In recent years, my company was faced with a number of critical decisions that I will share with you in this memo. In each case, we had the choice of following our competitors' lead or taking a different course of action entirely. My experience illustrates the importance of understanding your mission and devising your strategies accordingly.

Define Your Core Product or Service

The first issue we confronted concerned our core products, particularly life insurance. The life insurance marketplace is at a point usually described as mature, that is, stable but no longer growing as it once was. For many of our competitors, diversification to financial services was the answer. Investment products, fueled by the bull market, seemed a natural segue. The regulatory demarcations between banking and insurance were blurring. Many decided to branch out in new directions, becoming "One-Stop Financial Supermarkets."

We took a different view. After looking at everything carefully, we came to a number of conclusions. The life insurance market, though indeed mature, was large, dependable, and vibrant, producing $12 billion in new premiums annually. It was also a fragmented market with no single dominant competitor. Life insurance, unlike most other financial products, produced a continuing stream of income for our company. Our core competencies—actuarial, underwriting, and marketing—were perfectly suited to the marketplace we were in. And we had a distribution system of nearly 10,000 career life insurance agents that clearly differentiated us from other companies.

We knew we had a golden opportunity. Our competitors had lost their focus. In the scramble to enhance revenues with diverse products, they had taken their eye off the ball. So many of them followed the trend away from protection products and toward wealth accumulation products that they overcrowded the field of "financial services" while effectively leaving the life insurance market wide open. We decided that we would not follow the herd, but instead remain a life insurance company, focusing our energy and skills on taking an increased market share domestically and exporting our expertise to emerging overseas markets.

> IF EVERYONE HEADS FOR THE SAME
> GREENER PASTURE AT THE SAME TIME,
> THE NEW PASTURE TURNS BROWN AND THE
> ONE THEY LEFT BEHIND SOON STARTS
> LOOKING VERY GOOD.

Was it the right decision to remain a life insurance company? Time will ultimately tell. For now, I can tell you our increase in life insurance sales in the United States in 1999 outpaced the industry average by better than two-and-a-half to one. And our international operations are growing dramatically as we export our competencies. We are presently active in six countries in Asia and Latin America; we're the second-largest provider of individual life insurance in Mexico; and we anticipate being operational in the world's two largest markets, China and India, in the near future.

The lesson is a simple one: If everyone heads for the same greener pasture at the same time, the new pasture turns brown and the one they left behind soon starts looking very good. You, too, will have to make important decisions about what to focus your energy on and that of your executive team. You will have the added challenge of having the whole world's eyes on you when you decide you must buck the norm, as well.

Evaluate Your Resources Carefully

The second major decision involved our agency distribution system. Our competitors were abandoning their own agency forces one after another. They said an agency system was too expensive, that brokering and direct marketing their products was the way to go. We took a good, hard look at agency. Agency is an expensive distribution system: It literally costs hundreds of thousands of dollars to select, recruit, train, develop, and continue to educate a life insurance agent.

Was it worth the expense? We decided that if we could make the system more efficient and productive, it would be worth every penny. The old axiom is true—life insurance is not bought, it's sold. And the best way to sell it is through well-trained, highly motivated men and women who not only initiate the sale but also bring considerable added value to the

decision-making process. Agents begin the process by establishing a relationship with the prospect—one that may take years to
develop before a sale is made. They provide financial solutions
for a client's needs and goals, and then remain in touch to see
that the plan continues to work as the client's circumstances
evolve. No alternative system—direct mail, brokerage, the Internet—can replace that interaction.

Agents also provide an intangible asset of immense value.
Having a presence in almost every city and town across the
country, they project our brand image at the grassroots level.
Men and women come to know them, and through them to
know the company. You don't get that kind of identification
with brokerage or impersonal distribution systems. Our agents'
signs, offices, personal Web sites, local advertisements, and presence at community events are worth considerably more than
commercials during the Super Bowl.

Our research determined that our agents were indeed an
essential component of our business practices and products.
Instead of disbanding our agency distribution system, we
invested heavily in it. We asked agents and their managers what
they needed to be more productive. Then we explored and satisfied just about every item on the list. For several years now,
nearly every month our agents have produced more than they
did during the same month in the prior year. It's a trend that
shows no sign of abating.

Equally important and encouraging is our agents' commitment to a career in life insurance. Our continuing education
programs are working at full capacity. Our veteran agents are
mentoring the "rookies" in record numbers. Everyone's renewed

spirit is contagious. For 45 consecutive years, our agents have led the Million Dollar Round Table, the industry's premier sales organization, in membership, but our lead had been slipping before we decided to place our bet on our agents. Since then our lead has widened dramatically. No one is close to us and that bodes well for the future.

Here, too, the lesson is a simple one: If something of great value is broken, you don't throw it away, you can fix it.

Decide on Structural Issues

The third and most recent decision that had us bucking the norm involved our basic structure as a company. New York Life is a mutual life insurance company. In recent history many of our mutual company competitors, including MetLife, Prudential, John Hancock, and MONY, decided that they would be better off as stock companies. The move would give them access to capital markets that would provide funds to fuel their future growth. As a result of this environmental change in our industry, we were forced to weigh the pros and cons.

Life insurance is a unique product perfectly suited to the mutual company format. When people buy a life insurance product, they want to know that the company they bought it from will be here to pay the claim 20, 30, or even 50 years down the road. For 155 years, our goal has been to manage for our policyholders' future, to provide the kind of stability that life insurance demands.

Our corporate culture is oriented toward this financial stewardship; it's our primary role. Our perspective from day one has been long-term rather than short. Did we really want to put

ourselves in the position of having to focus instead on shareholder satisfaction and the stock market's quarterly expectations?

We didn't want to become a part of such a mercurial environment if we didn't have to. Unlike most of our competitors,
we had no need to raise outside capital to finance our growth.
(At the end of 1999, our surplus—or net worth—was $8.7 bil-
lion.) Once again, we decided to go our own way and *not*
change.

Here, again, the underlying principle is a simple one: A
corporate culture isn't something you *have,* it's what you *are.*
You can become better, more effective, more efficient without
becoming something else.

If it sounds as if these were easy decisions, however, I
assure you they weren't. In each case, we chose to ignore a
trend that our competitors had found irresistible, and did so
while still being responsive to consumer needs. We do make
and market our own successful line of mutual funds and asset
management products; and we do use secondary distribution
channels for those markets out of reach of our agents. But
essentially, we chose to remain what we are: an agent-driven
mutual life insurance company. In the year 2000, *staying the same*
in some ways *is* a very contrary notion. But solidifying rather
than collapsing our foundations has served us well. Our revenues are growing, our share of the industry is growing, and our
direction is clear.

The results of these decisions will guide us in the future,
but one thing is clear: while there may be safety in numbers,
sometimes the best course is to travel alone. Many of our com-

petitors have spread themselves too thin trying to be all things to all people. At industry meetings, more than one has expressed regret for abandoning the agency system. The IPOs that were supposed to have provided so much disposable cash have barely produced book value in many cases, and some will face the risk of takeover down the road.

As president of the United States, you are in a unique and powerful position, in fact, the most powerful position on earth. You will have untold influence on generations to come. I believe that you can do no greater service than to provide a clear and consistent vision—not one that is dictated by the latest poll—and let it be the template in guiding your cabinet and agency appointees.

LEONARD D. SCHAEFFER

Leonard D. Schaeffer is chairman and chief executive officer of WellPoint Health Networks Inc. Previously, he served as president of Group Health, Inc., and executive vice president and chief operating officer of the Student Loan Marketing Association. His government service includes working as administrator of the U.S. Health Care Financing Administration; Assistant Secretary for Management and Budget in the U.S. Department of Health, Education, and Welfare; and Director of the Bureau of the Budget for the state of Illinois. Mr. Schaeffer is a graduate of Princeton University.

WELLPOINT
HEALTH NETWORKS®

Leonard D. Schaeffer
Chairman & CEO

1 WellPoint Way
Thousand Oaks. California 91362
(805) 557-6000
Fax (805) 557-6100

MEMORANDUM

TO: President-elect of the United States

FROM: Leonard D. Schaeffer, Chairman
and Chief Executive Officer,
WellPoint Health Networks Inc.

SUBJECT: The Challenge of Leadership versus Management

Conventional wisdom holds that the "business of business" and the "business of government" differ such that the management skills of one do not necessarily translate to the other. Based on my experiences in the private sector and in several positions in both state and federal government, the management challenges in the private and public sectors are remarkably similar. How performance is measured, however, is very different.

In the private sector, there is an objectively defined "bottom line" which can be calculated at frequent intervals. Most private companies that consistently improve this measure are deemed successful. In government, other measures of activity or impact are used to assess management effectiveness. However, the president of the United States is not evaluated by the American people on his management ability.

While the president is held accountable for serious governmental operational problems, the president's most important accountabilities involve influencing individuals or institutions which are not in the president's formal chain of command and over which he has no formal management authority. Success in these areas cannot be measured by objective criteria such as GAAP.

THE PRESIDENT DOES APPOINT MANAGERS TO RUN MUCH OF THE FEDERAL GOVERN- MENT, BUT HE IS NOT A MANAGER HIMSELF. RATHER, HE IS A LEADER, ACCOUNTABLE TO ALL AMERICANS FOR THE COUNTRY'S FUTURE.

A president is evaluated on subjective criteria (other than in a time of war or great crisis) involving such things as the "quality of life" or "confidence in the future." The president does not have management authority over the economy or crime rates or how foreign leaders behave, but is expected to have effective influence in each of these areas and many more. The Congress, the federal reserve system, and the federal courts are parts of the federal government that do not report to the president, yet he must successfully impact these institutions if he is to be considered effective by the electorate.

The president does appoint managers to run much of the federal government, but he is not a manager himself. Rather, he is a leader, accountable to all Americans for the country's future. The president must express and effectively communicate a vision for the future and a set of values or decision criteria which guide his administration and can be used by others to predict his behavior and the policies he and his administration will promote at home and around the world. The president must convince the American people that his vision and his values are right for the country. In so doing, he causes people and institutions over which he has no management control to act in a manner that is consistent with achieving his vision.

THE PRESIDENT MUST CONVINCE THE
AMERICAN PEOPLE THAT HIS VISION AND
HIS VALUES ARE RIGHT FOR THE COUNTRY.
IN SO DOING, HE CAUSES PEOPLE AND
INSTITUTIONS OVER WHICH HE HAS NO
MANAGEMENT CONTROL TO ACT IN A
MANNER THAT IS CONSISTENT WITH
ACHIEVING HIS VISION.

Given the scale of the federal government and the enormous span of activities and issues on which the president is expected to act, he cannot personally reach all the people and organizations he must influence. Thus, the great presidents are not individuals who manage a group of followers through logical and persuasive communication of facts and ideas. They are symbolic leaders who embody and symbolize a set of beliefs, who convey their values through their behavior, and who inspire others inside government and around the world to act as they themselves would in a particular situation.

Symbolic leadership does require excellent communication skills and techniques, but first it requires a leader to refine his vision and beliefs to a relatively simple set of fundamental principles which can be (and are) applied consistently across issues and across time.

In order to lead effectively as our next president and to employ symbolic leadership when appropriate, you must first complete four important tasks:

1. Define and communicate your vision—provide a clear picture of the future to your administration, the American public, and the world.
2. Publicly describe and consistently apply your values and decision criteria when making important decisions—be a role model.
3. Embody your values in your daily life and use small events, everyday decisions, and symbolic occasions to demonstrate your beliefs and to inspire others to apply them in your administration and in society at large—use symbols and examples to inspire others.
4. Identify good managers who share your vision and values and appoint them to run your administration. Recognize, reward, and inspire them to achieve your vision.

Let your managers manage. You literally do not have time to manage the huge federal government bureaucracy. Ironically, the federal government does not include most of the important people and institutions you must influence to achieve your goals.

You should be focused on the future and on inspiring the people and important institutions in our country and all over the world to make decisions and act in a manner that will make your vision a reality.

JOSEPH NEUBAUER

Joseph Neubauer is chairman (since 1984) and chief executive officer (since 1983) of ARAMARK. He joined the company in 1979 and was elected president in 1981. Prior to ARAMARK, he held senior positions with PepsiCo, Inc., and Chase Manhattan Bank. He holds an undergraduate degree from Tufts University and a master of business administration degree from the University of Chicago.

MEMORANDUM

TO: President-elect of the United States

FROM: Joseph Neubauer, Chairman and
Chief Executive Officer, ARAMARK

SUBJECT: Building Your Team and Setting a Vision

Congratulations on your election as the next president of the United States. In your new office, you will not only be the leader of the free world, you will become the CEO of the largest "service organization" in the world.

I've been invited to make a few suggestions on how you might organize to deliver your agenda. I must say at the outset it is very humbling to offer advice to the leader of the free world. It is I who should be receiving counsel from you. But I will try to be helpful and will limit myself to a few fundamental issues that seem to be decisive in all organizations—private or public.

Build the Team

The first key to success in any organization is selecting the right management team and attracting the best talent at every level of the organization. This "war for talent" will be your first major challenge. As you know better than I from your own successful career in politics, it is not a war you can afford to lose. Drawing the best and brightest to public service today, particularly at the second and third levels of management where policy truly gets implemented—even shaped—will not be easy given record high levels of cynicism among the electorate, most notably among our young people. This is further complicated, at least at this current writing, by a booming economy which offers even modestly credentialed young men and women easy entrée into a vibrant global marketplace with the promise of quick and limitless rewards.

THE FIRST KEY TO SUCCESS IN ANY ORGANIZATION IS SELECTING THE RIGHT MANAGEMENT TEAM AND ATTRACTING THE BEST TALENT AT EVERY LEVEL OF THE ORGANIZATION. THIS "WAR FOR TALENT" WILL BE YOUR FIRST MAJOR CHALLENGE . . . IT IS NOT A WAR YOU CAN AFFORD TO LOSE.

If I may so suggest, you might want to do what many corporations are presently doing and have each of your departments and agencies create a council to:

- quickly assess your needs in all "critical hire" areas,
- evaluate best practices for screening, recruiting, developing, and retaining the talent that will be so important to your success, and

- assign accountability for the success of this initiative to a very able senior official.

You will also want to insist on regular progress reports and will need to give every indication at these meetings that this is an issue of great importance to you. You must communicate that you are holding the designated team accountable for delivering a critical mass of A-level talent.

At the same time, it is critical for you to show direct involvement in attracting and selecting talent. At ARAMARK, for example, I am personally involved in hiring the top 75 people in the company. In doing so, I have learned the following lessons:

- You must personally be part of the interviewing process for key managers.
- You must seek people who have different and diverse backgrounds from your own.
- You must be willing to take a chance on people.
- You must work to depoliticize the process.

It is only through personal, constant attention to the progress of this initiative that you can be assured you will win your fair share of the best available talent.

Set the Vision

The second key to success is to build a simple, defined, clear agenda and a communications platform that is equally clear and compelling in order to launch it.

It is a matter of no small challenge for you that words in the hands of elected officials today are viewed by many as tools of

deception. These are the instruments with which "spin" strategies are loosed upon targeted constituencies. This is a barrier
that you will have to face and overcome. But, like all barriers, it
is scalable.

People want to trust; and they *need* to believe. They know
all men—even powerful men like the president—are fallible.
They will, in fact, fail. They will disappoint. But when the mission is clear, and is perceived as "good," when it can be reasonably observed that the leader is focused and "channeled" in pursuit of a limited, and achievable, number of important goals, it
is much easier to marshal and sustain support through the inevitable difficulties and setbacks.

In corporations, employees at all levels need three fundamental messages continually reinforced:

- The overall vision for the enterprise, its fundamental business mission.
- The principle strategy, or strategies, through which the
  mission will be pursued and realized.
- How each individual fits—how, and why, what they do is
  important—within the overall context of the enterprise
  mission.

When the mission is cast as a larger "good," of noble purpose
(i.e., the advancement of freedom, the employability of the
underclass, the creation of economic value for customers, etc.),
and cast in very clear terms, repeated continually and with
emphasis—and, most important, wholly congruent with the
actions it summons—people follow. Most important, they will
"stay the course" when the going gets tough, as it inevitably will.

At ARAMARK, we developed a singular vision over the past five years called "Mission 10–5." It is focused on achieving five consecutive years of 10 percent growth. This year, we declared victory. Not only were we able to double our top-line growth, but we tripled profit growth as well. More important, we set a whole new standard of performance. We essentially created a growth culture that now permeates every group, district, market center, and component of our company, all around the world.

Create a "No-Limits" Culture

You will want to establish a "no-limits" culture and mind-set from day one of your administration. In other words all hands on deck must know, from the get go, that "good enough, isn't." Everyone must know that you are personally committed to achieving the highest imaginable standard of excellence in every area of your administration. They must also share in your covenant with the American electorate, which will require raising the bar in every area of the federal government's performance.

At ARAMARK, we recognize that every customer comes to us with a unique set of business practices. We work to create innovative and practical solutions that are customized to particular needs. Often this means doing things never done before. So we do them—without limits.

You'll find a "no-limits" spirit is contagious. If your people observe *you* pushing yourself, holding nothing back, putting yourself on the line at critical times, they will follow your lead.

If they see that you're imbued with a need to serve the needs and wants of others, they will follow. If they get a sense every time they are around you that adversity is a blessing, that

every cloud has a silver lining, that every problem has a solution, they will believe and follow your example.

If they can hear you calling them to a mission larger than
themselves, understand the benefits to others which will flow
from their sacrifices, and see you undeterred through trial and
adversity in pursuit of this "good," they will follow.

Of course you will not likely be able to get everyone on
board. But you'll have enough to form a critical mass of hearts
and minds, working together, however imperfectly, to deliver
something of significant value to others.

> IF YOUR PEOPLE OBSERVE *YOU* PUSHING
> YOURSELF, HOLDING NOTHING BACK,
> PUTTING YOURSELF ON THE LINE AT
> CRITICAL TIMES, THEY WILL FOLLOW YOUR
> LEAD . . . OF COURSE YOU WILL NOT LIKELY
> BE ABLE TO GET EVERYONE ON BOARD. BUT
> YOU'LL HAVE ENOUGH TO FORM A CRITICAL
> MASS OF HEARTS AND MINDS, WORKING
> TOGETHER, HOWEVER IMPERFECTLY, TO
> DELIVER SOMETHING OF SIGNIFICANT
> VALUE TO OTHERS.

Political realities will always and everywhere force compro-
mise upon you; you will become prudent. You will take what
you are given without compromising principle. Your people will
observe how you respond carefully. They will also observe you

relentlessly pursuing "the other half" of this greater good for others, tempered, always, by prudence, patience, and wisdom. In so doing, you will define, and continually redefine a "no-limits" mind-set in action as perseverance in adversity, hope amidst failure, and a deep abiding faith in the essential goodness of the American people.

Mr. President, thank you for taking the time to hear these simple suggestions. I do believe they have been tried and found true by very successful CEOs of major U.S. corporations. It is my hope that they will be of some help to you. Like all Americans, I wish you success as president of our United States.

2

MANAGING
CHANGE

JAMES J. SCHIRO

James J. Schiro has been chief executive officer of PricewaterhouseCoopers since its creation in 1998, upon the merger of Price Waterhouse and Coopers & Lybrand. Mr. Schiro has held various positions with Price Waterhouse and became its chief executive officer in 1997. He was appointed a member of the Independent Standards Board when it was created in 1997. Mr. Schiro is a graduate of St. John's University.

*Price*Waterhouse*Coopers* ⓡ

PricewaterhouseCoopers
1301 Avenue of the Americas
New York NY 10019
Telephone (212) 707 6470
Facsimile (212) 707 6444

James J. Schiro
Chief Executive Officer

MEMORANDUM

TO: President-elect of the United States

FROM: James J. Schiro, Chief Executive Officer,
PricewaterhouseCoopers

SUBJECT: Managing Change

> "Today our concern must be with the future. For the world is changing. The old era is ending. The old ways will not do."
>
> —*Senator John F. Kennedy, Acceptance Speech at the Democratic Convention, Los Angeles, July 15, 1960*

In the 40 years since John Kennedy surveyed the political, social, and economic landscape and declared the opening of a New Frontier, America has been transformed. Yet his words resonate with the unmistakable ring of truth, because the need to find ways to deal with change has only intensified. It's no exaggeration to say that there's been more change in the past 10 years than in the previous 100. While it took the better part of a century for the steam engine to transform the West from an agricultural to an industrial society, it took just over a decade for the Internet to propel us into the digital age. Largely driven by technological innovation, the pace of change—in business, in government, and in daily life—is accelerating. And so John Kennedy's words were prescient indeed: The old ways will not do.

The result is that America's economic might, once measured in smokestacks, assembly lines, and oil wells, now resides in the sum total of our ideas. We operate in a global, knowledge-based economy, and no company can long maintain its competitive edge unless it is willing to continually transform and reconfigure itself to meet new marketplace demands. As Charles Darwin observed, "It is not the strongest of the species that survives, nor the most intelligent, but the one most responsive to change."

Today's successful companies excel at developing and disseminating information. Consequently, the way organizations and people interact is undergoing a fundamental change. Companies of every kind are reshaping themselves, downsizing, and outsourcing their services. They're benchmarking their efforts against the best in their class, and they're working directly with clients (and sometimes even competitors) to improve efficiencies and achieve a greater competitive advantage in the marketplace. Speed and customer service are paramount.

Mr. President-elect, while the dizzying pace of technological change and the globalization of the economy are widely discussed, another related but little noticed transformation is underway. Citizens are rightly coming to see themselves as consumers of government services, and they are demanding the same level of responsiveness they have come to expect from the purveyors of goods and services in the private sector.

In every interaction between government and the people it serves, there is something we might call the "citizen-to-government interface." It has to be made seamless. It has to be made better and more functional. It has to be made more efficient. A government "of, by, and for the people" should feel that way and *work* that way. As the first president elected in the twenty-first century, your challenge will be to infuse the federal government with the kind of agility and responsiveness successful businesses exhibit. Should you succeed, you will have achieved a feat of lasting importance, because the role of the federal government will have been redefined for a new era.

> CITIZENS ARE RIGHTLY COMING TO SEE THEMSELVES AS CONSUMERS OF GOVERNMENT SERVICES, AND THEY ARE DEMANDING THE SAME LEVEL OF RESPONSIVENESS THEY HAVE COME TO EXPECT FROM THE PURVEYORS OF GOODS AND SERVICES IN THE PRIVATE SECTOR.

Change is never easy, especially in an organization as broad and complex and *tradition bound* as the national government. Making it better will take time. But there are many precedents. PricewaterhouseCoopers is also a large and complex organization with a long history and set of traditions. But, in a little more than two years, we have been able to change our firm and to do so utterly and on a global basis. There is much the government can learn from the way the private sector has embraced and—at times—resisted change.

Managing Change

In fact, PricewaterhouseCoopers has literally reinvented itself twice over since 1998. And so we are all change managers here. To seize the advantages of scale on a global basis, Price Waterhouse and Coopers & Lybrand merged to become PricewaterhouseCoopers in July 1998. In the months that followed, we integrated our operations to create a single, seamless global organization.

But market forces are relentless, and even before the final details of the merger were in place the changing business climate prompted us once again to restructure our organization by separating our business units into independent, stand-alone entities that could respond more fully to client needs.

If that weren't enough, while all this was going on we continued to help clients navigate through the same climate of accelerating change that we ourselves were experiencing. Today, as a result, we are more focused than ever on customer service.

Given our track record of managing change and the continuing dislocations wrought by the market, it is not surprising that our clients ask us, "How do you effectively manage change?"

There's really no short answer because every situation is unique. But I do believe there are many universal elements— best practices—which can be applied to almost any situation and will immediately improve the chances of success.

When we undertook our merger in 1998, we had the benefit of hindsight. We knew from our experience with clients that large-scale organizational changes are usually derailed by little things—words that are left unsaid, objectives that are never articulated, and questions that go unanswered. The devil truly is in the details.

Top Priorities: Communications

As our organizations came together, we made internal communications a top priority. We said we'd have no secrets, no surprises, no hype, and no empty promises. Through it all, we made a concerted effort to reach all of our people with news of what we were doing, to be as up front with them as possible about what we were trying to accomplish, and how it would affect them. The objective of this communications effort was to ensure that all our people were motivated and working toward a single goal. In short, we were seeking to inspire in our people the sense of "mission" associated with political campaigns.

> PEOPLE IN ANY ORGANIZATION . . . RIGHTLY WANT TO FEEL THAT THEY HAVE AN INVESTMENT IN THE ORGANIZATION AND BELIEVE THAT THEY SHOULD PLAY A ROLE IN MAJOR DECISIONS.

This is no easy task, particularly in a highly regulated business like ours. Earlier this year, for example, as we were negotiating the finer points of our restructuring with the Securities and Exchange Commission, there were times when we couldn't be as forthcoming as we would have liked with our own people.

But that didn't mean we had to maintain radio silence. At one point, we called our partners together in meetings all across the country and said to them point blank: "This is what we can tell you, this is what we can't. As soon as we can say something more, you'll be the first to know."

People in any organization—whether they are partners in a firm or staff members in a government agency—rightly want to feel that they have an investment in the organization and believe that they should play a role in major decisions. While soliciting wide-ranging input during the decision-making process is not always practical, timely and substantive communications from the leadership can do much to safeguard the cohesion of the organization during times of uncertainty.

Top Priorities: Focus

In our business, it is very important that our people not become distracted and lose sight of their clients during periods of change. So our merger strategy was centered on what we call "value drivers." These are nothing more than high-impact, high-probability-of-success actions that would get us where we want to be the quickest.

For instance, we said we wanted to energize and retain our best people during the merger. We took steps to ensure that everyone was working as productively as possible, that they had the tools to do their jobs, and could focus properly on key business objectives. It worked. Our retention levels actually increased during our merger.

Top Priorities: Cost Management

We asked our people to help us manage costs more effectively. And they did, by helping to eliminate redundancies within our organizations as they came together.

At the same time, we instituted procedures that would keep people focused on immediate objectives and growth. In fact, our service lines implemented 100-day business plans—that focused everyone on the most pressing issues of the day—while longer-term strategic priorities and plans were being developed.

Looking back on it all now, I can tell you that these value drivers really worked. They kept us all focused on our priorities. We didn't lost sight of our clients. Whenever we were faced with big decisions, we were able to put the question at hand to a true litmus test.

We would ask ourselves:

"Will this help us communicate better?"
"Will it help us retain our best people?"
"Will it help us manage costs and grow?"

Those that didn't stand up to the test, no matter how well intentioned, didn't make the cut.

One of our clients, who went through a similar transitional experience, put it even more succinctly. He said:

"If it doesn't advance a value driver, I'm going to shoot it, sell it, or ignore it."

Comparing Notes: Other Examples

One of the best examples of business transformation comes right in the federal government's own backyard. The U.S. Postal Service, one of our largest clients, has undergone an amazing transformation while competing against some of the most nimble, highly capitalized firms in the world, not to mention the advent of e-commerce.

Today, the Postal Service has taken dramatic steps to streamline its operations and upgrade service. Along the way, it has improved its bottom line. And it has become a leader in workforce development.

The private sector does not have a monopoly on change. Many world governments are doing some very innovative things in terms of improving efficiencies. For example, governments in Australia, Singapore, and the United Kingdom have developed advanced electronic procurement programs that would be worth studying and emulating in the United States.

Lessons Learned

So what can government learn from the business transformation experience?

The first lesson is the importance of paying attention to marketplace signals, and being able to interpret them in terms of your own situation. In our case, we knew from what we were seeing around the world that the dynamics of business were changing at a very fundamental level. If we wanted to be more successful in the future, it was clear that we would have to do things differently than ever before.

We simply had to become more innovative and more strategic in our thinking. We had to implement quicker and leverage our knowledge better than anyone else. We also had to become more intuitive in our ability to understand and anticipate marketplace needs.

The second lesson we learned is the importance of communications and focus. Sharing information on what's happening—what the outcome will be and why the transformation is happening—is critical. The less said, the more likely it is that people will lose their focus and direction. When that happens, clients are often the big losers.

The third lesson we learned is one that's easy to forget until you're actually going through it yourself—manage the details, but don't get bogged down in them.

Complex organizational transitions are inherently risky. Most fail to live up to their expectations, and the big reason why is because everyone gets so buried in paperwork that they lose sight of what they're actually trying to accomplish.

We found that the old "80/20" rule—which tells us that in most transactions, 20 percent of the tasks drive 80 percent of the value—can really help out here.

For us, the tasks were our value drivers. They helped us to define the most important things we needed to accomplish up front, the tasks and processes that created the most value.

Using this same principle, we were able to accomplish certain things while our merger was in progress that few believed were possible. For example, we were actually able to agree on a single audit methodology. And then we proceeded to train 60,000 assurance partners in this approach in 90 days.

But the most important lesson we learned about change really comes under the heading of "human nature." Whenever you bring cultures together—or ask people to change habits that have been ingrained for years—you have to tread carefully. As I indicated at the beginning of this memo, there are no off-the-rack solutions that will do the job for you. But you can dramatically improve your chances for success by taking fully into account the cultural differences and perceptions that will inevitably surface whenever you ask people to do things differently.

Cultural transformations are hard work. But they're well worth the effort, because even the best-laid plans and strategies won't work if your people aren't behind you.

Leadership

A philosopher once observed that when faced with change, people first deny it, then they vigorously oppose it, and finally they accept it as self-evident. A transition of this magnitude will incur mighty resistance—from entrenched interests hostile to reform and from well-meaning people who simply fear the unknown.

However, you will also find many allies within government, people with ideas and energy just waiting to be unleashed. Seek them out and assign them to the right tasks. Then limit resistance and increase your chances of victory by:

- Taking advantage of every opportunity to communicate.
- Planning carefully and focusing your efforts on high-impact objectives.
- Investing heavily in training and attracting people to the new paradigm.
- Helping top managers accept mistakes along the way, and getting past the inclination to develop "fail-safe" procedures or rules to engineer each and every controversy or issue.
- And I can't emphasize this enough—by being especially sensitive to the human element in your organizations.

The key to organizational change is getting people comfortable with shedding business-as-usual practices. This can't be forced from the top—you can't pass laws or rules mandating that people think differently. Organizational values, rewards, and motivations need to change. And above all, people in the organization need to recognize through their own good sense and examination that the new way is better than the old.

At this point in history, when e-government has become feasible and attractive for many functions, there is an opportunity to institute changes in government processes that are as momentous as are those now occurring in the private sector. By reshaping the federal government for a new century you will ensure that our founders' promise of a government of, by, and for the people is fulfilled for future generations. I know that business will support you in meeting this challenge.

WILLIAM R. JOHNSON

William R. Johnson joined H. J. Heinz Company in 1982 and held a variety of senior positions before being appointed president and chief executive officer in April 1998 and chairman in September 2000. Mr. Johnson has held a variety of senior positions, including vice president of Heinz, USA, president of Heinz Pet Products, and chief executive officer of Star-Kist Foods, Inc. Prior to joining Heinz, he held positions at Drackett, Ralston Purina, and Anderson-Clayton. Mr. Johnson holds an undergraduate degree from University of California, Los Angeles, and a master of business administration degree from the University of Texas.

WORLD HEADQUARTERS

600 Grant Street
Pittsburgh, Pennsylvania 15219-2857

William R. Johnson

MEMORANDUM

TO: President-elect of the United States

FROM: William R. Johnson, Chairman,
President, and Chief Executive Officer,
H. J. Heinz Company

SUBJECT: Leadership for a Changing World

Whatever their political agenda or social philosophy, America's most effective presidents have been those with a clear purpose and the strength and skill to take command of events—both expected and unexpected. The accelerating pace of change in the new millennium ensures that the world will be very different in four years. As a result, you will have to create and continuously revise a strategy for being a definer of change at the same time as you react to it.

Some leaders, such as Washington, Polk, Theodore Roosevelt, and Ronald Reagan, set out with clear objectives and an unwavering determination to achieve them. Others, like Lincoln, FDR, and Truman, found themselves in the midst of crisis, yet quickly seized the initiative and made an impact. All prevailed in the face of uncertainty and opposition. All adapted to circumstance but refused to succumb to doubt. All were determined to be drivers of change.

The experiences of today's business leaders, who have become, out of necessity, adept at managing change, will be helpful as you take on your new role. Because of the economic changes and technological innovations that have transformed the food industry, we have learned very quickly how to manage change. I would like to share with you some observations about leading change that I hope will be helpful to you in meeting the challenge of managing the federal government.

Change Must Be Quick and Pervasive

Change is at work everywhere, constantly redefining our environment and our constituencies. It is also far reaching, with each transformation generating multiple consequences. In such an environment, a leader who wishes to take command of change must act quickly and operate across a broad field. Hesitant, incremental actions are easily overwhelmed. Bold, broad initiatives alone can move an organization forward.

At Heinz, for example, we have had to contend with the new economic climate and investor expectations wrought by the rise of the technology industry. The so-called new economy has changed the rules and raised the bar for performance across all industries. Even though many unproven dot-com stock prices have begun falling back to earth and investors are beginning to take a more sober assessment of value, the economy boom has, at least for the time being, changed the financial landscape and what investors want. To meet that need, Heinz has swiftly and aggressively addressed the new investor expectations of rapid revenue growth, new market conquests, and strategic acquisition. Having achieved significant cost savings through restruc-

turing (in the range of $200 million per year), we are focusing
on revenue growth, aggressive innovation, and increased product consumption in both new and established markets.

The process of upping the ante begins with leading the
leaders. That means instilling in our management team around
the world the same enterprising zeal that led to the creation
and growth of the Heinz company 130 years ago. We have
altered our executive compensation to move from a largely
cost-focused culture to one that stresses top-line, as well as
bottom-line, growth.

We have had to also reassess our global marketing and product management strategies in order to align them with our new
goals. I have told our executives repeatedly that there are no
mature markets at Heinz, only mature marketers. As long as
change is endemic to our thinking, there are no limits to growth.

This philosophy is manifest in very concrete and specific
terms. We have made significant investments in innovative
packaging and edgy advertising to rejuvenate our established
brands, such as Heinz ketchup and Ore-Ida frozen potatoes. We
have launched new product ideas, such as Boston Market Home
Style Meals, to generate excitement in our core categories and
find new customers as they develop. More breakthroughs are on
the way.

Technology, too, is being employed, as we develop e-commerce capabilities to reduce costs, increase supply-chain efficiency, and enhance our business-to-business relationships
with our suppliers as well as our retail customers. We formed a
senior-level management team that is leading the charge on
e-commerce, enabling this "old economy" company to leverage

the power of the new economy to generate continued growth and improved performance.

Change Must Foster New Alliances and Open New Markets

We also have forged partnerships to drive growth in new, rapidly expanding markets. Through an alliance with The Hain Celestial Group, Heinz has made a major commitment to organic and nutritional foods—a veritable "dot-com" of our industry, growing at a 25 percent annual rate in the United States and Europe. Joint ventures in Indonesia and the Philippines have opened large and fast-growing markets relatively unknown to Heinz in the past. In turn, the new markets have transformed Heinz into a major player in Asian sauces—a segment whose popularity in the East we expect to replicate in Western markets, particularly among the rapidly expanding Asian-American population.

Such examples are consequences of Heinz's pervasive commitment to rapid renewal. They illustrate the response of one company's leadership to a universal challenge for business and government alike—continuous and constructive change. We have found that managing change requires great speed and aggressive action—two things for which governments are not noted in peacetime. This will be a major challenge for you.

Change Must Be Relevant

As John Wooden, the great UCLA basketball coach, once observed, "All progress requires change, but not all change is progress." Effective leaders do not initiate change for its own sake. They use change to address major trends and issues that shape the needs and desires of their constituents.

Our global consumer experience has led us to note several universal trends that are likely to shape tomorrow's political and commercial environment. We believe that every organization, including yours, can benefit from paying attention to the "4 Ts" as outlined below.

- *Teens: The Next Generation.* There are some 800 million teenagers around the world, and they are using the latest communications technology to fashion a global culture of their own. American teens have more in common with teens in Japan or Italy than they do with middle-aged adults in their own country—a reality with powerful political and economic implications. Additionally, for the first time in history, the younger generation has dominance over the primary factor driving our economic growth. It has complete knowledge and experience when it comes to technology. For this and many other reasons I think you should be acutely aware of the needs and desires of young consumers and young voters (education, employment, entertainment, etc.) and you must consider the global implications of those aspirations.
- *Travel: An Emerging Global Environment.* Young and old alike are part of an increasingly mobile society. Ideas and people are constantly in motion. Trends and causes in the farthest corners of the world rapidly migrate, mutate, and move on. In our daily lives, we are constantly on the go. In my industry, this accounts for the dramatic growth of

away-from-home eating, particularly in North America
and Europe. Our leadership in the foodservice segment
depends on our ability to offer creative product and packaging solutions for an increasingly mobile market. A similar imperative exists for all organizations, including yours.
As more people, products, and ideas travel internationally,
they force the removal of artificial political barriers as
well. I believe that you should encourage this process
through policies and actions that enable the free flow
of information, capital, and trade as well as consider the
many massive implications of emerging globality—both
economic and social.

- *Time: The Need for Speed.* The more people move, the
  greater their need for speed. Consumer-friendly is the
  order of the day and the driving force in our service-
  oriented society. Here, too, the Internet has accelerated
  gratification and elevated expectations. For all organizations, including the federal government, convenience,
  speed, and ease of use must be factored into any new
  product configuration. Within our industry there are
  direct examples of a market need. Home meal replace-
  ment has become a major trend, as food companies look
  to provide a growing menu of high-quality, great-tasting
  products that require minimal preparation. Shopping habits, too, are evolving as options for increased ease and
  speed are opened by e-commerce. You, too, will be
  afforded with the technology to enable you to provide
  taxpayers with a more service-oriented, user-friendly
  government.

- *Talent: The Competition for Great People.* One of the most
  significant challenges for leaders of all sectors is the competition for talent. Although the United States has become
  a haven for the highly skilled, we have no room for complacency. The mobility of the world's population dictates
  that people will go to where the opportunities are. As
  Heinz has seen in its global affiliates, there is a world of
  opportunity for talented people. The challenge for our
  leadership is to allocate human resources most effectively
  on a global scale. We have combined our North American
  operations to facilitate the transfer of talent on this con-
  tinent. But we also are employing global management by
  product category to break down geographic and affiliate
  barriers within our company and enable the rapid movement of talent and the speedy transfer of best practices
  around the world. You will play a crucial role in maintaining a favorable and competitive climate for attracting
  human as well as financial capital. Just as the United
  States depends on foreign investment, so it must remain a
  magnet for global talent in order to sustain growth in a
  tight domestic labor market.

The wants of future generations, the emergence of a new
global marketplace, the need for speed, and the competition for
talent are major factors driving change throughout the world.
They are challenges to effective leadership in government and
business. They will certainly reshape businesses such as Heinz
over the next four years, and they are likely to alter the economic, social, and political environment of the United States

as well. To lead change successfully, you will have to manage these dynamic factors and anticipate their influence. You will have to prepare to continually refine the structure of government to be more responsive to these influences. Above all, you should work with business organizations to leverage these trends to generate growth, excitement, and opportunity in the years ahead.

Change Must Be Personal

As we take stock of the global environment, we must not forget that the impact of change is felt one person and one community at a time. All marketing, like all politics, is local. Even ubiquitous brands such as Heinz ketchup must adjust their marketing methods and sometimes even their recipes to local tastes.

> AS WE TAKE STOCK OF THE GLOBAL ENVIRONMENT, WE MUST NOT FORGET THAT THE IMPACT OF CHANGE IS FELT ONE PERSON AND ONE COMMUNITY AT A TIME.

A key effect of change today is the growing empowerment of individuals. Technology has given ordinary people extraordinary access to information. It has created new alliances and communications networks among investors, consumers, and interest groups. As leaders, we must resist the new pressures that arise from this open environment. The constant flow of new information can lead to a ceaseless "play-by-play" media analysis of every minor move leaders make. Successful leaders—public and private—must steer their organizations steadily forward in pursuit of their long-term vision. We may allow for adaptation as circumstances arise, but we must not stray from our ultimate goals.

Rather, we should use the power of the new technology to open new channels for engaging our key publics with direct and continuing dialogue. Business leaders now can speak personally to shareholders and investors via Internet Webcast, delivering our messages without the traditional filters of analysts and media. We also can use sophisticated market data and analysis to understand our consumers on a very personalized basis and establish lasting relationships through highly targeted marketing programs. Such tools are already employed in election campaigns. But you now can continue the direct dialogue throughout your tenure and use it to lead the nation one citizen at a time.

As the leader of the United States, you will have a unique relationship with the people of this nation. You can use that relationship to encourage change, to unleash creative energy, and to leverage the power of technology. You will also have a new opportunity to reach out to the rest of the world—to be a leader to a new, global generation that is young, technologically sophisticated, and highly mobile.

Change is a powerful tool. I ask you to use it prudently and with a full understanding of the best interests of our country—both as a nation of free people and as a participant in a greater global economy. In that context, I would leave you with the famous prayer of St. Francis of Assisi: "Lord, grant me the courage to change the things I can, the serenity to accept the things I can't, and the wisdom to know the difference."

WILLIAM D. ZOLLARS

William D. Zollars has been chairman of the board, president, and chief executive officer of Yellow Corporation, one of the largest transportation service companies in North America, since 1999. Prior to that, he was president of Yellow Freight System and senior vice president of Ryder Integrated Logistics. He also spent 24 years as an executive at Eastman Kodak. Mr. Zollars holds a bachelor of arts degree in economics from the University of Minnesota.

William D. Zollars

Chairman of the Board
President and Chief Executive Officer

MEMORANDUM

TO: President-elect of the United States

FROM: William D. Zollars, Chairman of the Board,
President, and Chief Executive Officer,
Yellow Corporation

SUBJECT: Deploying Technology and Changing Culture

The greatest challenges facing your new administration will be
your ability to deploy technology to build more effective customer relationships and to change culture in the diverse and
numerous organizations that comprise the executive branch.
Though you were elected with a mandate to bring change to
the halls of government, we both know that will not be an easy
task. With that in mind, I'd like to share with you my experiences in deploying technology and changing culture in a rapidly evolving industry.

In the world of trucking-related transportation services,
change has not come easily. Even though Congress deregulated
the industry in 1980, real competition did not emerge until a
few years ago. While customers (and the economy) have benefited from better service, more choices, and competitive prices,
some of the older and more established trucking companies
have really struggled with the transition.

During the first decade of deregulation, financially strong companies like Yellow had little difficulty in the face of competition. They continued to grow simply by picking up business left by the weaker players as they went out of business. But that cycle had ended by the early 1990s. At that time, the industry entered the final stages of deregulation, which lasted until about 1996. This period was marked by severe price discounting, the end of intrastate regulation, and disruptive labor strikes. Many carriers struggled, including ours, and quite a few "old guard" companies were driven out of business.

At the dawn of a new millennium, our industry has finally taken control in this competitive era. With just a few exceptions, the companies that are left are financially strong, battle-tested, and offer greatly improved service. Customers are justly expecting more and more from their transportation providers and receiving better service as a result.

The challenges facing your cabinet and other members of your executive team will be similar to these current business dynamics in some important ways. The federal government is a large buyer and seller of services. As service providers, we face nearly identical challenges in utilizing the potential of the Internet to create new efficiencies in supply-chain management and better channels for delivery of products and services. And we each face the challenge of how to strengthen our relationships with our customers—in your case the American people.

Deploying Technology to Build Relationships in a New Business Environment

Businesses today operate in an unprecedented way in this demand-driven environment. Point-of-purchase information drives decisions in retailing, manufacturing, and most segments of the supply chain in between. This type of constant change means that a competitive advantage today may not be a competitive advantage tomorrow. With product life cycles now measured in weeks instead of years, speed to market is key. You had better be able to have a new product on the shelf or on the Web very quickly. And it's equally important to be able to turn on a dime, exiting quickly when conditions change.

The key to a sustainable competitive advantage for most businesses today is having a well-oiled supply chain. This requires strong strategic partnerships with many parties, including manufacturers, distributors, and transportation partners. In fact, the transportation relationship may be the key to making the whole supply chain work. The need to form fast and powerful alliances is shared by all industries and businesses today. I have no doubt that the same will be true for organizations within the federal government.

With the explosion of e-commerce in the digital age, the complexity of the supply chain for most businesses (both bricks-and-mortar and virtual) has increased by a factor of four or five or more. Supply chains—sourcing networks and distribution channels of all sorts—now stretch around the globe. With the increased number of relationships that must be managed, many logistics and procurement professionals are simply overwhelmed. The companies that learn how to take the pressure off these individuals and work as true strategic partners will have sustainable competitive advantages themselves.

Building Important Relationships. Building strong business relationships can be tough. An effective partnership is like a marriage, where good communication, listening skills, and flexibility are mandatory. The relationship is a dynamic learning process that begins when each party agrees to listen and to do their best to understand what the other has to say. Many companies boast about their strong customer relationships but the reality is that there are very few solid ones in our industry. Good customer relationships can be very fragile things.

> WHILE IT'S VALID TO FOCUS TECHNOLOGY
> INVESTMENT ON COST SAVINGS OR
> OPERATING EFFICIENCY, THE RETURNS
> BEGIN TO DIMINISH IF THAT INVESTMENT
> IS NOT ALSO IMPROVING THE CUSTOMER'S
> OVERALL SERVICE EXPERIENCE.

Do we have to accept the reality of delicate relationships as a fact that can't be changed? Absolutely not. Technology is changing business dynamics at warp speed, giving us new methods to dramatically improve these all-important relationships. That, in my opinion, is the most dramatic result of an investment in technological advances. While it's valid to focus technology investment on cost savings or operating efficiency, the returns begin to diminish if that investment is not also improving the customer's overall service experience.

Simply using technology does not create a competitive advantage for a transportation services provider, or any business for that matter. Focusing technology investment on simply maintaining legacy operating systems is a losing strategy. At Yellow, we practice the "2-to-1 Rule." For every dollar invested in legacy system support, we invest two dollars in development of new systems and technology. In addition to employing the "2-to-1 Rule," we avoid programs and projects that take more than three years to complete. The entire industry has moved on by the time those projects are finished. Your cabinet secretaries would certainly benefit from challenging each of their chief information officers to tell them whether the "2-to-1 Rule" is applicable to the federal government in general and each of their departments specifically.

Reaching Untapped Markets. In our industry, the Internet will not relieve existing pressure to engage in commodity-based transactional pricing. When a buyer simply wants commodity service, price drives the buying decision. From airline tickets to home mortgages, the Internet lets buyers comparison shop like never before. A certain amount of price-driven comparison shopping is inevitable in the digital marketplace for transportation of products and materials. There are many transportation services companies willing to function within that business paradigm. The low-cost business model does have its place in every industry.

However, transportation services providers who believe that we will inevitably return to the days of one-size-fits-all commodity service, with uniform and highly discounted pricing, are missing the real potential of the Internet. That was a defining characteristic of our regulated era. Today, the digital age is giving us the power to customize service and manage relationships like never before, offering alternatives to price-driven buying.

That's the business model Yellow has adopted. We believe that the Internet actually will open up vast untapped markets for value-added services that will be much larger than the relatively small pond we fish in now. The total market for transportation services, including air freight and rail is around $440 billion today. The sector in which Yellow presently competes represents approximately $26 billion, or 6 percent of the total. But the sector can hardly be described as a commodity service market anymore. Our research shows us that less than one-fourth of our customer base makes purchase decisions based on price alone. The remainder say service quality is the most important factor when choosing a partner.

Thanks to technology, we now have the ability to say "yes" to the manufacturing manager who has 16 shipments that must be picked up at the same time and then must each move to different parts of the globe at varying speeds and finally be delivered to the consignee within a one-hour time window. You can't meet demands like that with commodity service.

Increasing Accountability. Technology has to be placed into the hands of the people on the front lines who have the best chance of using it to create, maintain, or strengthen a positive relationship with the customer. The investment can't stop with giving your people better tools. You also must deploy technology that gives your customer better access to information that in turn helps them manage their own business. It may be information about a shipment moving through our system, a status report on an invoice, or advice on filling out a bill of lading or customs documentation. Whatever information the customer needs, we have to be ready to provide it in real time. It's increasingly true that our ability to move information is just as important as our ability to move products and materials.

The technology revolution in our industry has raised the threshold of accountability. It's increasingly difficult to make excuses for poor or erratic service. The slipups just don't get past the customer anymore. By giving the customer the ability to track shipments and retrieve documentation, chronic problems stand out pretty quickly. Yellow is giving customers an unprecedented level of control over their shipments while they move through our network so that potential errors can be derailed. Shipments that are in danger of being late can be sped up or rerouted or even returned. Offering compensation to customers experiencing problems is an important counterpart of this service. Within our industry, the idea of giving our customers choices and then holding ourselves accountable with guarantees was nearly unheard of in the past. Today, technology is driving more and more companies to hold themselves accountable for the quality of service they provide.

Changing the Cultural DNA

The technology revolution requires a dramatically different corporate culture. But changing an existing culture is one of the hardest things any company can do. It is essentially changing a company's DNA. It can't be done in a month or two. It requires constant and relentless attack over a long period of time. You and your new appointees will face this challenge if you truly desire to change the culture of your organizations.

The first thing you have to do in order to transform a culture is to defeat complacency by creating a sense of urgency. In doing so, you need to be careful not to create anxiety. People don't function well in an environment ruled by fear. They either burn out, run for the exits, or just do everything in their power to sabotage your efforts. A sense of urgency means giving people clear direction and expectations, setting aggressive goals, and then establishing a generous reward system for meeting the goals. They must feel like participants in a joint mission. Implementing this strategy at Yellow has resulted in a real turnaround on our bottom line.

The next important step is to adopt a clear and simple vision for where you want to go as a company. At Yellow, we started this process three years ago by articulating that we wanted to be the leading provider of guaranteed, time-definite, defect-free, hassle-free transportation and related services. Earlier this year, we recognized that the vision wasn't as clear and easy to understand as it should be. So we refined it by engaging in a little self-analysis and asking ourselves: "What is our core purpose as a company?" We agreed that our core purpose is simply "to make global commerce work by connecting people, places, and information." We believe that statement reflects the essence of our vision.

Communicating the Vision. The next important step in changing the culture is to relentlessly and repetitively communicate the vision to employees. The rule of thumb in advertising is that a selling message must be repeated at least three times for it to register with a potential buyer. That principle also works in communicating important messages to employees. Communication is a difficult, but necessary task in both the public and private sectors.

Communication must start at the top with a management team that connects the dots for employees. They must show employees the bigger picture and put every necessary change and activity within the larger context. They must constantly ask: "Is this move consistent with our vision? Is this where we want to go as a company?" With enough repetition, employees begin to internalize the vision and test the consistency between it and their daily actions on an ongoing basis. No doubt, civil servants, like those in my organization, also seek to understand the bigger picture. In addition to spending time outside of their organizations—talking to constituents, interest groups, business, government, and Congress—your cabinet secretaries and agency heads must also allocate time to communicate your vision of a better government with their own employees.

Creating Short-Term Wins. It's also important for morale and long-term productivity to create short-term wins. By establishing interim goals that can be achieved quickly, employees begin seeing that their efforts are paying off. At Yellow, that effort was centered around a company-wide process improvement program in which best practices were identified throughout the company, taken apart and reengineered, and then institutionalized across our entire network. In so doing, we have the opportunity to turn our best minds loose to truly innovate.

Our "Gold" processes were the result of that effort. They have established benchmarks of efficiency and predictability for every important activity involving the movement of 15 million shipments per year. The Gold processes create short-term wins that every employee can see and relate to. They are an important base to build on as we now move to other activities that will improve the overall service experience for each customer.

Empowering Employees. An effective culture also must have a structure that supports the strategy to strengthen or change it. One of the biggest fallacies in business today is the idea that any organizational structure will work as long as good people are in place. Talented people alone won't get a job done. The truth is that winning organizations have superior people operating within a superior structure. In 1997, as part of our effort to reinvent our company, we radically reshaped our entire management and organization structure. Our goal was to move decision-making authority closer to the customer and to get more people involved in bringing innovative ideas to the table.

The final element in creating real change in a culture is to reinvigorate passion. Vince Lombardi once said: "The difference between a successful person and others is not a lack of strength, not a lack of knowledge, but rather a lack of will." That idea holds true for organizations, too. Pride and passion are the foundations of willpower. People have a competitive fire that makes them want to succeed. They want to be proud of what they do. When you demonstrate to them that they have reason to be proud and the ability to impact results, they will supply the passion. If you reward incentive, you will keep passion alive.

It's been a long road for the people in our company, through deregulation and into an era of competition ruled by the power of the marketplace. Technology is the tool that has helped us emerge as a completely new company positioned to thrive and prosper in the digital age. It is inevitable that the change that new business dynamics has enforced will have a profound impact on how you and your executive team choose to handle internal and external relationships, culture issues, and redefinition of your own business models and goals.

EDWARD A. BLECHSCHMIDT

Edward A. Blechschmidt is chairman, chief executive officer, and president of Gentiva Health Services, a public company launched in 2000 as a split-off from Olsten Corporation, where he was chief executive officer. Previously, Mr. Blechschmidt was president and chief executive officer of Siemans Nixdorf Americas and Siemans' Pyramid Technology, and also worked for more than 20 years with Unisys Corporation. He holds a degree in business from Arizona State University.

Gentiva
HEALTH SERVICES

Edward A. Blechschmidt
Chairman & Chief Executive Officer

175 Broad Hollow Road
Melville, NY 11747
631 844 7220
631 844 7538 Fax

M E M O R A N D U M

TO: President-elect of the United States

FROM: Edward A. Blechschmidt, Chairman,
Chief Executive Officer, and President,
Gentiva Health Services

SUBJECT: Leading Change to Fulfill Your Strategic Vision

Some 2,500 years ago, the Greek philosopher Heraclitus observed that "the only constant is change." It was a simple statement, but it still holds true today. Change is inevitable and continuous. Whether one is president of the world's most powerful nation or head of a corporation, executive leadership is, more than anything, a matter of leading change.

Of course, successfully managing change also means recognizing its risks, and they are numerous. For example, change can sometimes run the risk of proving overwhelming to organizations and their personnel. There are human-cost factors to consider, such as the risks of turnover, loss of productivity, and damage to the trust and loyalty that associates feel toward the organization. Change can also be frightening.

But to successfully lead change, executives must diligently avoid these pitfalls because the positives of leading change almost always outweigh the potential negatives. Managed properly, change can lead to renewed focus and passion, new processes, realignment of resources, and organizational efficiency. Nor is change something that can simply be ignored. Organizations that recognize change as the path to enhanced productivity, relevance, and prosperity place themselves on the road to success. Those that do not make that recognition place their organizations at the risk of irrelevance and, ultimately, failure.

These factors hold true for all types of businesses. But in the health care industry, they have proven especially so. Driven by shifts in demography, technological developments, government regulation, and economics, health care has been in a state of rapid change since the implementation of managed care in the 1980s. In recent months, this change has proven even more rapid. The message to the health care industry has been clear: lead the process of change or be overwhelmed by it.

At Gentiva Health Services, we have been working to align our business with these changing trends. For nearly 30 years, Gentiva Health Services has been one of our nation's leading providers of home health care services. Through nearly 400 locations, our network of caregivers provides health services to more than 450,000 clients each year. Our customers include managed care organizations, government agencies, hospitals, and individuals. At Gentiva, we believe that home health care is a vital part of a seamless, cost-effective system of health education, preventive care, and therapy. It is the vision on which our business is based and upon which we have staked our future.

The Origins of Change

Like many companies, Gentiva started as a small operation and has grown into a much larger one. Today we are a $1.5 billion

corporation. Because our growth came primarily through acquisitions, this led, over time, to an amalgam of disparate cultures,
systems, and operating processes. Each business unit had its own
forms and procedures. At one point, our nursing division alone
used multiple computer billing programs. Communication among
various Gentiva businesses was fragmented, inconsistent, and
unorganized. There was no common mission, brand, or technology platform, no single telephone access number for customers.

A large organization cannot continue indefinitely without
adopting a unifying strategy and mission if it is to remain competitive. We realized that our only viable solution was to undertake a far-reaching effort to get all our businesses moving in the
same direction. We called this project Re-engineering Enterprise-
wide Operations, or REO. Under this banner, we utilized change
as a method to reach our strategic operating goals and our mission to improve the health and well-being of our patients and
their families.

> A LARGE ORGANIZATION CANNOT CONTINUE
> INDEFINITELY WITHOUT ADOPTING A
> UNIFYING STRATEGY AND MISSION IF IT
> IS TO REMAIN COMPETITIVE.

During the 18 months it took for this project to be completed, we executed sweeping changes against an aggressive
time frame. One of our executives likened this undertaking to
"having open-heart surgery while running a marathon." We
created standardized, enterprise-wide manuals covering opera-

tions, staffing, intake, and other areas while vastly simplifying customer access. New training and performance-measurement programs were developed and we put the entire company on a single e-mail platform to improve communications.

Key Factors in Leading Change

Working as a team, all our associates at Gentiva learned valuable insights from this project. The key for our organization was to learn to embrace change. Change is not something to avoid at all costs. It is a tool to leverage and bring about results. Our organization now feels that if we're doing everything this year the same way we did last year, then we're doing something wrong. We also learned that to successfully lead change you need to measure what you monitor, and if you want people to resolve a problem, it must have associated action items designed to address those issues. Here are some key factors that were helpful to us in effectively leading change:

Clear, reasonable, goals and expectations. Organizational change will not succeed without clearly defined and quantified goals. People must have an end point in sight, and a sense of how much effort is needed to get there. It is important to set deadlines, and hold people accountable to meeting them. It is equally important not to saddle people with more initiatives than they can reasonably be expected to handle at the same time.

Strong project management. Organizational reengineering is a machine with many moving parts—and, not surprisingly, enormous potential for destructive friction. Well-defined work plans and strong project-management discipline are vital. At Gentiva, the creation of a centralized project-management office reflected our belief that there had to be someone at the controls who could coordinate and synchronize essential parts with an eye on minimizing intrusions into field operations.

Effective and honest communication. Organizational change can be unsettling and even destabilizing, and is guaranteed to create anxiety in the workforce. To minimize the negative impact, regular, clear, and honest communications are essential. From the outset, we resolved not to let our people feel powerless, or deceived. We took pains to tell them exactly what was in store, what was in it for them, what was expected of them, and what their options were. We did this through a variety of dedicated newsletters, meetings, conference calls, Web sites, and feedback forums. We also spent a lot of time on the "campaign trail" reinforcing the key messages.

Rewards and recognition. We knew that it would take hard work on the part of a small corps of committed individuals to accomplish meaningful change. We determined from the outset not to take their efforts for granted. Simple expressions, such as a congratulatory voice mail or handwritten note of appreciation for a job well done, go a long way toward motivating continued commitment and high performance.

Speed. Reengineering shouldn't last forever. To succeed, it's important to move fast—not just because of competitive pressures, but also because speed conveys urgency. Setting deadlines is a powerful motivator. When change initiatives are permitted to drag on, they invariably lose momentum and grind to a halt.

Fact-based decision making. Gut feelings have their place, but organizational change is too complex to be entrusted to intui-

tion alone. Decisions should be rational, never impulsive. And
they should be informed by facts that are gathered through sta-
tistical research, through interviews with customers and associates, and by other means.

Active risk management. No sooner does an initiative get
under way than the conditions on which it is based begin to
shift. Sponsors and champions of a project may leave the company and be replaced by managers with different priorities.
Unanticipated regulatory changes, acquisitions and divestitures,
competitive moves, and even political events can radically alter
the landscape and render your plans obsolete. Thus, we learned,
success requires that you scan the horizon for events and developments that may undermine your resources, or otherwise force
you to alter your goals and strategy.

Lessons Learned

Organizational change not only takes an enormous amount of
planning and anticipation, but it is also an opportunity to learn
new things, and rethink old assumptions. Consider some of the
lessons we took from our experience:

Lesson #1: Buy-in begins at the top. For change to succeed,
it must have the blessing of anyone with the power to affect
the destiny of the organization. But executive buy-in has to go
beyond a mere nod of approval. Each senior manager must fully
support the project charter and its goals, and understand precisely what he or she must invest in terms of support and energy.
Ideally, a senior manager's compensation should be tied to the
success of the initiative. What's more, everyone should be on
the same page. Without a focused effort to achieve alignment,

the initiative can fall victim to conflicting executive priorities and marching orders.

Lesson #2: Promote associate ownership. It's always better to empower your people to change rather than to mandate it. While mandating change may seem a shortcut to a goal, we found that associates are more receptive to and enthusiastic about change when they actively participate in its development and implementation. Change initiatives have a better chance of acceptance by people who feel empowered. All things being equal, people prefer autonomy to directives.

Lesson #3: Celebrate success. The ultimate success of any large-scale enterprise is made up of many smaller, transitional successes. Celebrating those milestones with parties, awards, bonuses, and letters of commendation goes a long way toward sustaining commitment over the long haul.

As a corporation, we define success by criteria such as profitability, revenue growth, capital strength, and customer satisfaction. I strongly believe that these factors are every bit as applicable to national governance as they are to private enterprise. To paraphrase Calvin Coolidge, the business of America is still business.

Our nation has always embraced change. We have searched for new ways to do things, and once we found them, we have sought ways to further improve upon them. As we begin the new millennium, the opportunity to foster change as a catalyst to enrich all our lives has never been greater. At Gentiva Health Services, we have applied this catalyst by using change as a force for realizing our strategic objectives and for providing "Care You Can Count On" to the thousands who need it.

ERIC KUHN

Eric Kuhn is president, chief executive officer, and cofounder (in 1997) of Varsity Group Inc., a premier college marketing company and on-line retailer. Mr. Kuhn previously practiced real estate and corporate law in Miami, Florida, and in New York City. Mr. Kuhn holds a bachelor of arts degree from Haverford College and earned a law degree from the George Washington University Law School.

MEMORANDUM

TO: President-elect of the United States

FROM: Eric Kuhn, President, Chief Executive Officer, and Cofounder, Varsity Group Inc.

SUBJECT: The Importance of Knowing and Understanding Your Customers

You know as well as anyone that we are in the midst of a time of significant change. Rapid technological advancements are impacting both the public and private sectors to such a degree and at such a pace that our ability to manage and leverage these changes will largely determine our success or failure economically and socially. Internet usage alone is proliferating at an unprecedented rate—outpacing the adaptation to previous communication innovations, such as TV and radio. The Internet has made our world a smaller and more efficient place to work, communicate, and live—and has opened us up to an entire new realm of possibilities.

In December 1997, I founded VarsityBooks.com, an Internet company that pioneered selling discounted new college textbooks. I wanted to bridle the power of the Internet to bring efficiency and cost savings to the college market. By adapting new technologies and new business models to a traditional market, and by creating a grassroots network of over 2,000 on-campus student marketers nationwide, we have been able to become a premier on-line destination for college students. We have since become an important marketing partner to companies that want to reach this sought-after demographic. Our rapid growth is one example of the new speed of business in general. The Internet, with its increased efficiencies, has allowed business to be conducted at a faster pace. We have to keep up with the public's resulting desire for more, better, and faster. That mandate is not limited to business, but to all entities that serve the general public, including the federal government.

Scanning the Environment

As CEO of Varsity Group Inc., I am constantly evaluating the environment as it changes at breakneck speed. Based on this environmental scan, I'm constantly making necessary adjustments. In conducting this scan, I ask myself several key questions to help assess the landscape and to make sure that my business is keeping up with our competitors. I believe that your cabinet secretaries and agency heads might find it useful to ask these very same questions.

How Are My Customers Changing? First, I look at the constituencies we serve as a company to see if their needs, wants, and expectations have changed. I ask myself if consumers in general are asking for more variety, better customer service, or a different product than they were in recent history, and then we determine if our offerings answer these new needs. In order to better understand the demands of my constituents, I try to determine why their needs have changed—Is a change being affected by a new technology or a current event? Once we have determined whether or not needs have changed and why, we must decide how our company will respond. Your agency heads face these same issues in dealing with their customers, the American public.

Varsity Group Inc. has tried to respond to a growing set of constituencies. For example, in the beginning, we focused solely on bringing students a better, more affordable way to buy their textbooks. Since then, as a result of our growing expertise, developed in marketing to college students, we have broadened our customer base to include companies seeking to reach this demographic through our on-line and off-line marketing services. It is a priority of mine to continue to bring students products and services that make their everyday lives better, as well as to now offer our marketing services to all companies who want to fully penetrate this market. This, in turn, will build a solid relationship with both constituencies. I believe that as time goes on we will not only form stronger relationships with our current customers, but our constituency base will expand to include others. The trick is to start with your most direct market and work your way out. If you have credibility with your primary constituency, others will follow.

Are My Competitors Changing? Another way we assess the environment for reaching our goals is by looking at our competitors. If they are changing their business, then we must ask ourselves whether or not they are changing in response to real or perceived needs of the customer—and whether or not we think they are moving in the right or wrong direction. When making such an assessment, it is important that our competitors are properly defined. In your case, your executives face a challenge in determining exactly who their "competition" is—is it other federal agencies, state or local government, or the private sector which can now assume some activities previously carried out solely by government?

> BRICKS-AND-MORTAR COMPANIES ARE FAST LEARNING THAT MORE AND MORE CONSUMERS DESIRE THE SAME TYPES OF PRODUCTS, DELIVERED VIA NEW TECHNOLOGY. LIKEWISE, THE SERVICES OF THE FEDERAL GOVERNMENT WILL HAVE TO BE MADE AVAILABLE THROUGH METHODS THAT PROVIDE INCREASED EASE OF USE AND SPEED.

Varsity Group Inc. does not want to be all things to all consumers. We want to be the number-one brand for the college demographic and the leading college marketing company. We keep that mission in mind when evaluating the actions of our competitors, who may have a different business goal.

How Do We Tailor the Core Business So That It Is Competitive and Effective? Are we still providing what our customers need and in a manner in which they need it? Bricks-and-mortar companies are fast learning that more and more consumers desire the same types of products, delivered via new technology. Likewise, the services of the federal government will have to be made available through methods that provide increased ease of use and speed. Certainly, it seems that the IRS is a terrific example of a technologically modernized federal agency, as more and more taxpayers are filing online every year.

Responding to the Changing Environment

Based on the conclusions revealed through answering these basic questions, we must begin to respond accordingly through improved systems, methods, and offerings where necessary. In order to adapt our business, we must be prepared to implement these changes quickly. There are several key characteristics that allow us to make such adjustments to best respond to the market and to our constituents.

Make an Elephant Think Like a Gazelle: Remain Agile. For any organization, but especially in these times, it is critical to move more quickly and accurately. At Varsity Group Inc., we organized ourselves around a central goal and set out to orchestrate a sequence of several quick strikes. As a business that must respond to technologies moving at light speed, it is important that our business does not operate on a model that requires changes on a global scale at a glacial pace. By coordinating smaller, faster efforts, we are able to make the changes most necessary first while moving toward larger objectives.

In our early days, our small size afforded us the luxury to make quick decisions and act immediately. As the company has

grown, it is more difficult to change directions as quickly as
before, but that capability remains equally important.

AS A BUSINESS THAT MUST RESPOND TO
TECHNOLOGIES MOVING AT LIGHT SPEED,
IT IS IMPORTANT THAT OUR BUSINESS DOES
NOT OPERATE ON A MODEL THAT REQUIRES
CHANGES ON A GLOBAL SCALE AT A GLACIAL
PACE. BY COORDINATING SMALLER, FASTER
EFFORTS, WE ARE ABLE TO MAKE THE
CHANGES MOST NECESSARY FIRST WHILE
MOVING TOWARD LARGER OBJECTIVES.

We have organized our company to focus on bringing
both students and companies seeking to reach students the
best possible products and service. And we achieve that goal
through a series of simultaneous steps. At all times, there are
designated teams that focus 100 percent of their efforts on a
certain customer. We have teams of employees that are solely
focused on bringing client companies the maximum results
from their relationship with Varsity Group Inc.'s on-line and
off-line marketing services. And, at the same time, we have
teams of people directly focused on the retail part of our business that targets students directly. The creation of teams is
important in order to allow us to remain successful in growing
larger and gaining more market share in the short time allotted
for reaching our goals.

The importance of remaining swift and nimble is not, how-ever, eclipsed by the continued importance to remain strategic. Our quick-strike efforts made possible by our agility are always guided by an overall strategic plan.

Do More with Less: Maximize Resources. As an Internet start-up, we have had to put thoughtful time and energy into devel-oping ways to maximize our limited resources.

Human capital: Our most valuable asset. After we decided to move forward with our vision of transforming the college text-book market, I immediately realized that we needed like-minded visionaries to help us realize our dream. As we interviewed can-didates, we sought out those people who shared our passion to revolutionize a market and provide value to every college stu-dent. You will face the challenge of choosing your team to carry out your objectives and the challenge of inheriting employees who will need to understand your vision and mission.

Recruiting and retaining individuals who understand and share our commitment has been a critical element of our suc-cess. Because the Internet is a young industry, there are few experts who can tout multiple years of experience working in this environment. We therefore surrounded ourselves with experts from all walks of business—and with those people who share our vision.

Equity in the vision: Our most unique asset. In the beginning, I wanted to hire the best, brightest and most motivated to join our company, but as a company we were limited in what we could offer new employees. We had to figure out how to maximize our resources to create a compensation package that would provide enough incentive to attract this caliber of employees. Thus, we began to offer our employees a stake in the business they were creating—a financial incentive to keep alive our vision. Equity quickly became one of our most important recruiting tools. All Varsity Group Inc. employees are partial owners of the company. No matter how large or small that stake, the very notion gives employees a sense of personal accountability that is unique to ownership. It is clear that whether it is shared vision or shared financial responsibility, team-oriented values will help to motivate employees to continue to serve the consumer.

While we can attract employees with financial equity, we retain them with equity in the company's direction. Every senior manager, myself included, abides by an open-door policy, so that every employee can be invested in the future of the company. We all believe that every idea deserves consideration, and therefore keep our doors open to every employee so that they can be heard. Further, we empower our employees with responsibility to an extent that may go against conventional corporate wisdom. We have a young, aggressive, talented staff that demands their compensation extend beyond the paycheck and into their minds. As managers, we are tasked with constantly finding new ways to engage and stimulate our staff. The goal in providing all types of equity to employees is to empower them with a feeling that their work—their daily tasks—can make a difference.

Technology. Clearly, as an Internet-based company, we have seen the power in creating efficiencies through technology. Yet, it remains our challenge to leverage technology to enhance all facets of our business. It will be the same for you. The bottom line for any business is based on the ability to attract and retain customers, or "loyal followers." Businesses and government agencies alike can benefit from enhanced communications provided us through the Internet. Now, we can communicate with our constituents more frequently and more consistently due to the increased efficiencies brought by the Internet. At Varsity Group Inc., we use on-line and off-line communications with our customers to provide them information on their order status, give them special offers and, perhaps most important, get feedback on their buying experience with our company, and to provide them with a human face behind our Web site and service offerings. Our open line of communication helps us better address our customers and gives them a better sense of who we are as a company. It is those technologies that led consumers to rank us as the leader in customer confidence as reported in Gomez Advisors' Spring 2000 Internet Bookseller Scorecard. We are proud of that accomplishment, because we think that customer confidence is hard won in the age of technology, where so many products and services are available at our fingertips.

We have also turned technology on ourselves to enhance employee communications and facilitate collaboration. Using technology, we are able to better coordinate our efforts across multiple business units. Our communications structure makes sure that we are not duplicating efforts and basically keeps the right hand informed on the activities of the left hand.

See the Forest Before the Trees: Maintain Vision. It is no secret that I am passionate about Varsity Group Inc. and our

mission to become the premier college marketing company.
Through efficiencies brought about through new technologies,
we are able to effectively communicate that mission to our staff
and to our customers. We know who we are, as do the constituencies we serve. All decisions are weighed against our core
mission to reach every student every day. We think about it, we
work it, and we live it. As you determine your objectives and
your cabinet secretaries and agency heads determine theirs, it
will be crucial to communicate those goals to your constituencies, and have them participate actively in pursuing those
goals.

DO NOT UNDERESTIMATE THE IMPORTANCE
OF SIMPLY HAVING FUN ON THE JOB, AND
PROVIDING EMPLOYEES WITH THE OPPOR-
TUNITIES TO BECOME INVESTED IN YOUR
LONG-TERM GOALS.

In summary, I would encourage you to share with your
executives some of the lessons that I have learned by creating
Varsity Group Inc.:

- Regularly scan the environment to better understand the
  changing needs of your customers.
- Respond to the changing environment by structuring your
  organization so that it can easily adapt to change.

- Use the resources—technological, human, and financial—
  you have to their maximum potential.
- Finally, do not underestimate the importance of simply
  having fun on the job, and providing employees with
  opportunities to become invested in your long-term goals.

3

LEADING
PEOPLE

J. W. MARRIOTT, JR.

J.W. Marriott, Jr., is the chairman of the board (since 1985) and chief executive officer (since 1972) of Marriott International, Inc. He joined his father's Hot Shoppes restaurant chain full time in 1956, and soon took over management of the company's Twin Bridges Motor Hotel in Arlington, Virginia, Marriott's first venture into the lodging industry. Mr. Marriott graduated from the University of Utah in 1954 with a bachelor of science degree in banking and finance.

 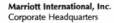

Marriott International, Inc. Marriott Drive
Corporate Headquarters Washington, D.C. 20058

J. Willard Marriott, Jr.
Chairman of the Board
and Chief Executive Officer
301/380-7511
301/380-8957 Fax

M E M O R A N D U M

TO: President-elect of the United States

FROM: J. W. Marriott, Jr., Chairman of the
Board and Chief Executive Officer,
Marriott International, Inc.

SUBJECT: The Importance of People

At first glance, a large private-sector enterprise like Marriott
International might appear to have little in common with the
federal government. Not only are we driven by different forces—
profit versus policy—but we answer to very different audiences:
Marriott, to the marketplace; the government, to taxpayers and
the Congress of the United States.

Such fundamental differences aside, we do share a number
of challenges. Among other things, both of us manage huge and
diverse workforces. Both must deal effectively with hundreds of
contractors and partners. And both operate in thousands of
locations across the country and around the world. Above all,
we have a common mission: serving the public. Our customers
look to us to fill a need, solve a problem, or otherwise make a
difference in their lives. In Marriott's case, the challenge might
be as straightforward as providing a clean and comfortable

room for the night. For a federal agency, the request could be vastly more complex. Whatever the situation, our success as organizations rests in large measure on one critical factor: our people. We depend upon employees who thrive on helping others. Who see problems as opportunities. And who can't rest until a solution has been found.

> HUMAN BEINGS LIKE LEADERSHIP. EVEN IN THESE DAYS OF FASHIONABLY "FLAT" ORGANIZATIONS, EMPLOYEES WANT TO KNOW THAT SOMEONE IS FIRMLY IN CHARGE AND THEY WANT TO MAKE A DECISION ABOUT WHETHER OR NOT THEY WILL FOLLOW THAT VISION. . . . HANDS-ON MANAGEMENT HAS BEEN TALKED ABOUT TO DEATH IN THE PAST 20 YEARS, BUT THE TRUTH IS, IT WORKS.

Finding the right people to meet the demands of our organizations is always a challenge, but perhaps never more so than today. Like virtually every American employer, public or private, we face one of the tightest labor markets in recent memory. The "boomers" are heading toward retirement, leaving in their wake a much smaller workforce. With fewer people available to fill jobs, employers need to be more responsive than ever to the needs of those who choose to work for us. We can't afford to bring good people on board, only to lose them because we haven't taken steps to ensure their satisfaction and well-being on the job.

Fortunately, keeping and cultivating a great team of people is not a mysterious process, and although you yourself might not be directly involved in hiring all those who will be your employees, you will be able to set the standards for those who will. A grasp of human nature and a little institutional elbow grease are the main requirements for those who manage people. As my father, J. Willard Marriott, Sr., often observed: "Take care of your employees, and they'll take care of your customers." With that plainspoken wisdom in mind, let me share a few road-tested rules of thumb that have guided us at Marriott for three-quarters of a century.

See and Be Seen

Human beings like leadership. Even in these days of fashionably "flat" organizations, employees want to know that someone is firmly in charge and they want to make a decision about whether or not they will follow that vision. I don't mean that person must be simply running the business, developing strategy, and making the big decisions—important as those tasks are. I mean that the leader must be visible at the helm. Hands-on management has been talked about to death in the past 20 years, but the truth is, it works. Long before textbooks touted the practice, my dad spent thousands of hours every year visiting with Marriott associates, getting to know them and listening to their problems and insights, in the process knitting the company's far-flung workforce into a single corporate family. Although the company has grown exponentially since my father's day, I've tried to follow in his footsteps—both literally and in spirit. I can't offer empirical evidence that what I do makes a difference, but I have absolutely no doubt that every mile I travel pays for itself in staff morale, commitment, and company spirit.

> PEOPLE NEED TO HEAR [GRATITUDE] ON A DAILY BASIS, WHEN THEY'RE ACTUALLY IN THE TRENCHES, NOT SIMPLY WHEN THEY'VE ACCOMPLISHED SOMETHING OUT OF THE ORDINARY OR ANOTHER 12 MONTHS HAVE ROLLED BY. HOW DO YOU MAKE SAYING "THANK YOU" INFECTIOUS? LEADERSHIP BY EXAMPLE.

Know When Rules Are Meant to Be Broken

We take a lot of kidding at Marriott for our minutely detailed procedures and quality control checklists, but I can't imagine life without them. By giving our staff a road map for getting the job done, every Marriott associate in every business unit understands what needs to be accomplished to maintain our standards, our values, and our goals. That's no small thing when you're trying to get 146,000 people all over the world to march in one direction. But it's equally important not to let a penchant for process get in the way of the real goal: solving a customer's problem. Standard operating procedures take care of many difficulties—maybe even most of them—but there will always be situations that call for a jolt of initiative and imagination. At

those times, employees need to know that stepping outside of
the rules to find a solution will bring congratulations, not criti-
cism. How to get the message across? Begin by championing customer-driven thinking. Follow through by giving employees the
resources and latitude to do what they need to in order to take
care of their customers. And finish with recognition and rewards
for those who go the extra mile. You will need to figure out ways
that you can put your special stamp on rewards, so that the message that you are aware of the extra efforts gets through.

There Are No Thankless Tasks

Old-fashioned courtesy sometimes gets short shrift in our fast-
paced world. That's a shame, because saying "thank you" is one
of the easiest ways to make people feel appreciated and good
about themselves. One method of showing gratitude, of course,
comes in the time-honored form of monetary reward. But appreciation should not be limited to an annual raise or bonus. Nor
to special awards and honors. People need to hear it on a daily
basis, when they're actually in the trenches, not simply when
they've accomplished something out of the ordinary or another
12 months have rolled by. How do you make saying "thank you"
infectious? Leadership by example. And making sure that everyone on the team understands how everyone else's contribution
lightens the load for all.

Give People Something to Stretch For

Basic human psychology tells us that we're more likely to do
our best when we're challenged. That's hardly surprising. People
like to feel good about what they do. After all, who takes pride

in a mediocre job? But high standards don't simply materialize out of thin air. Someone has to set the tone. When my parents went into business more than 70 years ago, they placed a premium on superior performance. Whether the task was polishing silverware, or serving hot and cold food, any job worth doing was worth doing not merely right, but superbly, to the very best of the doer's ability. Although the company is now many times larger than either of them ever envisioned, their ethic of excellence remains one of our core values. I also think it's one of the qualities that attracts people to come work for us . . . and to stay, often for many years.

Encourage the Spirit to Serve On and Off the Job

Jobs in public service tend to attract people who are naturally pumped up by the chance to interact with and offer service to others. At Marriott, our corporate culture has been around so long and is so strong that we've given it a name: "the spirit to serve." And the spirit isn't limited to work hours. In spite of juggling jobs and families, many of our associates actively seek opportunities to volunteer in their communities.

To make it easier for them to reach out to neighbors, our company-wide "Spirit to Serve Our Communities" program helps our associates connect with a wide variety of volunteer work close to home. It's a classic win-win for everyone. Not only do our communities benefit, but our associates as well. Besides the satisfaction of helping to improve the quality of life in their hometowns, they often learn new skills that serve them well on and off the job. And the company values the chance to become more involved in the communities where we do business.

Help the Helpers

Serving the public is exhilarating. But it can also be exhausting. Especially if you're trying to deal with problems of your own. Here's where my dad's "Take care of your employees . . . " philosophy shines. Organizations that actively help their workers cope with problems on and off the job have a leg up over any organization that lets its employees struggle with family and life issues alone. At Marriott, we've taken my father's credo and created a 1–800 Associate Resource Line to which our U.S. employees can turn at any time to find help with anything from childcare and transportation emergencies to legal and counseling services. Of course, not every associate will need to use the hotline, but having it sends a powerful and positive message to every present and prospective employee about the company's commitment to the well-being of everyone who works for us.

Listen, and Then Listen Some More

My final point is not so much a professional, as a personal, rule of thumb. That motto is to listen as much as you can. People often expect leaders to do all or most of the talking, but you can't learn much if you're always the one on stage. During almost 50 years in the "people" business, I've learned the most valuable four words that any leader can utter, any day of the week, any time of year: "What do you think?"

ARTHUR M. BLANK

Arthur M. Blank is president and chief executive officer of The Home Depot. Mr. Blank cofounded The Home Depot in 1978 with Bernie Marcus. Prior to the forming of The Home Depot, Mr. Blank was employed by the Los Angeles-based Handy Dan Home Improvement Centers in financial capacities, including Vice President-Finance. Mr. Blank received a bachelor of science degree in business administration with distinction from Babson College.

Arthur M. Blank
President and C.E.O.

MEMORANDUM

TO: President-elect of the United States

FROM: Arthur M. Blank, President and
                    Chief Executive Officer, The Home Depot

SUBJECT: Managing in a Values-Driven Environment

As you view the responsibilities that lie ahead for your administration, I feel privileged to share some insights about how to
build a foundation for successful leadership. Whether you are
serving as president of a company or as president of the United
States of America, you know that your enterprise is as good as
the people within it, and the people are as productive as you
allow them to be.

With our 21 years experience at The Home Depot behind
us, I respectfully offer the following observations for your consideration.

**Your Selection of People to Cabinet Positions and Top
Political Posts Should Be Values-Driven Appointments**

Finding the right people for the most important jobs means,
first and foremost, attracting those who share the same basic
values upon which you base your most heartfelt and momen-

tous decisions. Once you bring them in, you must encourage them to express their individual points of view.

By values, I mean those core beliefs about how people should treat one another and what it means to do the right thing—beliefs that also include and honor differences in politics, religion, background, ethnicity, geography, and cultures.

My passion for values springs from our experience of building a great company from scratch. Our company was founded on values I shared with my partner Bernie Marcus. Several years ago we finally formalized them as eight core values. They are:

- Excellent customer service
- Taking care of our people
- Building strong relationships
- Entrepreneurial spirit
- Respect for all people
- Creating shareholder value
- Doing the "right" thing
- Giving back to our communities and world society

These values are the fabric of our company, the heart of our customer-service culture. As our company is expected to grow to 245,000 associates by the end of the year 2000, we have to ask the question, "How do we communicate and reinforce our values to our associates today, and to the many tens of thousands we will hire in coming years?"

One way to express values in a solid way is through formal programs. New associates learn about our values during orientation, and we continually reemphasize the strength of our values to our associates, to investors, to suppliers, and to other public audiences. Living our values is also the focus of the 360-degree review process we employ—which invites input from supervisors, peers, and subordinates—and is a key element in determining advancement and in succession planning.

Another and even more powerful way we communicate our values is by role modeling. Our standard for associates is to not only know the values, but more important to live them—to let them guide our decisions and actions, and to role model the values for others. What associates see their peers and leaders *do* gives meaning to what we *say*. This principle of human nature applies in all organizations, public and private, large and small.

Your cabinet and top political appointees should truly care about people, not just in words but more important in deeds. All decisions—in government as in business—affect people. Those who are appointed to areas of responsibility must carry inside them a special sensitivity to the short-term and long-term impact of their decisions on the circumstances, hopes, and dreams of their fellow citizens.

Finally, your cabinet members and top political appointees must take to heart the idea that as stewards of our government, their primary goal is to serve the people. One key to our success at The Home Depot is that our people at all levels, as stewards of this enterprise, know their primary goal is to serve our customers.

In Times of Rapid Change, Trust in Your People Becomes More Important

Once you have found the very best people, trust them to do what is right.

In the private sector, trust is the dominant force that moves an enterprise ahead. With the right value system and the right knowledge to do their jobs, people can be trusted to make the right decisions. Operating with this kind of trust means that your organization can more easily adapt to change, and even lead change. Managers feel no need to micromanage. And people will do more good for the organization than could ever be dictated.

> TO ENSURE THAT GOVERNMENT CAN MEET INCREASINGLY COMPLEX CHALLENGES, YOUR CABINET MEMBERS AND TOP POLITICAL APPOINTEES WILL NEED TO DEVELOP LEADERS WHO WOULD BE CAPABLE OF REPLACING THEMSELVES—WITH PEOPLE WHO ARE EVEN BETTER THAN THEY ARE.

For this reason, trusting people—allowing them to take risks, experiment, and make mistakes—has become a hallmark of The Home Depot culture.

When appointing company officers to my "cabinet," I seek people that I trust will bring knowledge and attributes that we need in order to strengthen the entire team. And as we continue to grow, recruiting and retaining top management become ever more critical to our future success.

To ensure that government can meet increasingly complex challenges, your cabinet members and top political appointees will need to develop leaders who would be capable of replacing themselves—with people who are even better than they are.

At The Home Depot, our charge to all levels of management is to identify and develop replacements who will be more adept, smarter, and more knowledgeable than they are, because our business is becoming more challenging and complicated with every passing year. As CEO, someday I will replace myself with someone more capable than me, because our evolving business will demand an even higher level of ability.

Your cabinet and top political appointees should also have a greater capacity than what you need today from them, in order to be ready to meet the increasingly complex challenges of tomorrow. They must be always "in class," seeking new knowledge and insights. In order to make the right decisions, they must continually learn more about the issues facing our country, and about innovative solutions that are on, or just over, the horizon.

Your top political appointees will help your administration adapt in a positive way to shifting realities of our world— changes in economic conditions, policy, demographics, culture, and public opinion—all of which can work toward or against the goals you envision for the country. In being flexible, however, your people must also have the wisdom to know what to change and what not to change as emerging problems and tasks continually test their expertise, resolve, and core values.

Communicate with, Care about, and Motivate the People in Your Organization

When it comes to work, all people are motivated by the same seemingly simple, strong desire—they want to do a good job and they want to be respected for doing it. A primary role for new cabinet members is to set a vision that honors the work their people do and then to communicate that message to everyone within their respective agencies.

TO STAY GROUNDED ABOUT THE OPERATIONS
AND PEOPLE IN THEIR AGENCIES, EVERY
CABINET MEMBER AND AGENCY HEAD
SHOULD ALLOCATE A CERTAIN NUMBER OF
DAYS PER YEAR TO VISIT WITH EMPLOYEES,
BOTH AT HEADQUARTERS AND IN THE FIELD.

My "cabinet," consisting of executive vice presidents, senior vice presidents, and vice presidents, helped set our vision of "leading the marketplace toward a better world." Through their decisions, communications, and actions, they provide that same direction to their functions, divisions, and store managers.

A vital part of that message for cabinet members and your top political appointees is how their agencies are finding and advancing the best people within the civil service. As newly appointed leaders, they must embrace the diversity of job candidates who can help their agencies succeed, then put in place the needed tools to advance and develop them. To stay grounded about the operations and people in their agencies, every cabinet member and agency head should allocate a certain number of days per year to visit with employees, both at headquarters and in the field.

We at The Home Depot believe so deeply in the importance of on-site visits that we require all officers and all members of our board of directors to work in or visit a certain number of our stores every quarter. I personally visit about 100 stores each year. There is no shortcut to this experience. Listening to associates gives one a clear understanding of how things are working and what needs to be improved. The visits also send a clear message to associates that their leaders stay informed about the business.

Finally, your cabinet and top political appointees will carry the American spirit in their hearts and a global commitment in their minds. In order to make the best decisions for their country, and the world society at large, they must wear metaphorical glasses that help them see the big picture.

As our lives become closer, faster moving, more complicated, and more interrelated, we also become more dependent upon and vulnerable to each other. The right people must understand that we are, ultimately, citizens of our world as well as of our great country, with a responsibility to each other.

SIDNEY TAUREL

Sidney Taurel is chairman of the board, president, and chief executive officer for Eli Lilly and Company. He became chief executive officer in 1998 and chairman of the board of directors in 1999. He joined the Lilly subsidiary Eli Lilly International Corporation in 1971 as a marketing associate. Mr. Taurel graduated from École de Hautes Études Commerciales in Paris, France, and received a master of business administration degree from Columbia University.

Sidney Taurel

Chairman of the Board,
President, and Chief Executive Officer

Eli Lilly and Company
Lilly Corporate Center
Indianapolis, Indiana 46285 U.S.A.

MEMORANDUM

TO: President-elect of the United States

FROM: Sidney Taurel, Chairman of the Board,
President, and Chief Executive Officer,
Eli Lilly and Company

SUBJECT: Leading People in Large Organizations

As the federal government has grown in size, cost, and complexity in the years since World War II, successive administrations have vowed to make it "more productive" or "more efficient" or "more responsive to the needs of the taxpayers." Efforts toward these objectives have tended to focus on programs, budgets, and agency scope and structures, with mixed results at best. No president, to the best of my knowledge, has ever focused on improving the performance of government by tapping the full potential of the *people* who work in it.

This "people" avenue is neither obvious nor glamorous, to be sure, and it is filled with formidable obstacles. As we all know, decades of accumulating work rules and other forms of bureaucratic protection have put most federal jobs safely beyond even the president's reach. But, precisely because it has gone so long untended, this domain holds the potential for the greatest productivity gains. Management, after all, means managing people. To make your mark as a true leader and a great manager, I would urge you to press for dramatic reform of, first, the rules and, ultimately, the culture of the federal civil service.

Moreover, the time for such an ambitious reform may now be at hand. Today, we have extremely low unemployment. In fact, the primary threat to our ability to maintain strong growth and low inflation may be the dwindling labor supply. Therefore, making government workers more productive would clearly enhance our national economic well-being. Increased productivity would be good for workers, good for taxpayers, and good for wage payers as well. Everyone wins.

Assuming the public system can be modified and you can begin to borrow some of the best practices from other organizations, the many dedicated and hard-working employees in the government may discover that the changes are actually exciting and rewarding. That's what our own experience would suggest.

> TO MAKE YOUR MARK AS A TRUE LEADER
> AND A GREAT MANAGER, I WOULD URGE YOU
> TO PRESS FOR DRAMATIC REFORM OF, FIRST,
> THE RULES AND, ULTIMATELY, THE CULTURE
> OF THE FEDERAL CIVIL SERVICE.

We at Lilly have learned a lot about tapping the potential of people in our 124 years of doing business. Over time, our philosophy of employment has earned us numerous awards and a reputation as one of the best companies to work for in all of industry.

And we credit our track record of bringing breakthrough medicines to patients in need, and our enviable growth in annual earnings over the course of our history, to our investment in people.

The employment philosophy at Lilly centers around the concept of "reciprocity." In the ideal scenario, a company will stretch—going above and beyond conventional expectations—to meet the needs of employees. And, in return, employees are expected to stretch to meet the needs of the company. The concept of reciprocity is a deceptively simple idea—with complex effects—that has evolved over many years. It exists more as a tradition for us than a traditional rule-bound system.

Nevertheless, I can point to some key principles from our practice that might serve as an outline of a guide for other employers, including the federal government. I offer them to you in hopes that they may have some value to you in your new role as "employer in chief."

Principle One: Hire the Very Best People You Can

For Lilly, this is axiomatic. The rate-limiting factor in our growth is not plant and equipment nor capital; it is talent, brainpower. We accept no compromises in going after the best and brightest people because they are the foundation of our business.

I fully believe the federal government can and should compete with private industry for good people. The notion that government should make do with underachievers is counterproductive. Moreover, the very high recruitment standards of many areas of government speak for themselves. Consider the difficult admission standards in our nation's military academies or the challenge of the Foreign Service exam. In the field of health care, we know first hand the exceptional caliber of talent in the Centers for Disease Control (CDC) or the National Institutes of Health (NIH).

I don't believe that most taxpayers think of these high standards—the State Department, CDC, NIH—as the norm in the federal government. Other agencies could profit greatly from those that represent "best practices" within your own government. An effort has to be made to change the existing view among the general public so that the government can recruit from among them.

Principle Two: Provide the Resources and Support Necessary to Help Great People Grow

At Lilly, we have established employee development as management's number one priority. We make a deep and systematic commitment to ensure that our people continually acquire, extend, and renew the skills they need not just to maintain but actually grow their value to the organization.

We hold all supervisors formally accountable for how they coach, develop, and communicate with the people they lead. This puts a very heavy charge on our managers to look ahead and:

- determine what skills will be needed as their business evolves;
- assess their people in terms of their possession of those necessary skills; and
- develop a plan and line up the resources to make sure everyone is acquiring the right skills for the right jobs, at the right time.

On the employee side of the deal, we expect them to take responsibility for continuously learning, continuously updating their skills to meet the ever-changing needs of the business. In the end, the concept of reciprocity has proven effective: we grow the people to grow the business. You can find exemplars of this principle in the federal government. The U.S. Armed Forces may be the most sophisticated and successful trainers on the planet. The proof of this is in how much military training boosts the future employability of those who receive it. The learning capacity achieved by the exemplary organizations in the military should be more widely emulated throughout the entire civil service.

IN PARTICULAR, FEDERAL EMPLOYEES SHOULD BE SYSTEMATICALLY TRAINED TO MUSTER AND DEPLOY ALL THE TOOLS EMERGING FROM THE INFORMATION REVOLUTION, BECAUSE THESE TOOLS HAVE ENORMOUS POTENTIAL TO IMPROVE EFFICIENCY.

In particular, federal employees should be systematically trained to muster and deploy all the tools emerging from the information revolution, because these tools have enormous potential to improve efficiency. Above all, I hope you can instill in your administration a sense of exploration and innovation with these new technologies to create for the federal government the kinds of productivity breakthroughs that are now transforming private industry.

Principle Three: Help Employees Balance the Demands of Work and Their Lives

Lilly has received a good deal of attention for the things we're doing to enable our people to make a life as well as a living. In recent years, we have initiated a wide array of work-family programs to try to help our people cope with new needs. These run the gamut from flexible work arrangements to childcare help to various on-site service facilities. These aren't perks or bribes. These are tools, designed to remove distractions and barriers to the performance of our people. We want all their energy and focus and creativity, while on the job, to be focused on the job.

Some of our programs might seem inappropriate in a government setting; administrators would surely have to be aware of how such amenities would look to Congress and to taxpayers. But any organization can and should take a realistic look at anything currently getting in the way of employee productivity, and take reasonable steps to eliminate such obstacles wherever possible.

Principle Four: The Relationship Between Employer and Employee Is Always a Two-Way Street; the Efforts Must Be Truly Reciprocal

You have to ask people to deliver results, and to meet tangible, measurable goals that move the organization on an upward path. To keep it moving upward, you must ask them to stretch and keep beating their own best effort.

In our performance management process—which, among other things, governs pay and promotions—we demand nothing less than continuous improvement in job performance of everyone in the organization, in every year of their employment. If this sounds like an onerous requirement, you'll have to take my word for it that what it really is is an expression of faith—faith in the deep, untapped potential that most people have within them. The interesting result is that the exceptionally high-potential people not only accept this challenge, they push back and ask for bigger challenges—support for greater personal risks—in order to grow as fast as possible.

Any organization that wants greater efficiency and productivity must emphasize results and must be prepared to deal effectively with those who cannot or will not deliver. Rightly or wrongly, I think most taxpayers have the perception that it is very hard to deal with poor performers in government service, and that consequently, few administrators really try, with the end result being that the federal ship carries much more "ballast" than any industry could tolerate. We at Lilly have found that *motivation* is much more carrot than stick.

The concept of reciprocity takes reward beyond merit pay. We try to reinforce the commonality of interests of all Lilly employees by pushing the idea of stock ownership and gain sharing much more broadly than most companies typically do. We believe that everyone's motivation can be fortified by being given a stake in the results.

This last concept—insisting on continuous improvements in results and tying rewards to achieving them—is the one I think the federal government needs most. But it may also seem like the one that would be hardest to adopt. The government, after all, doesn't make profits and cannot issue stock to give employees ownership in the venture. Nonetheless, a variation on the private sector theme seems doable.

Bureaucracies—whether in the public or the private sector—tend to perpetuate inefficiency by defining and measuring work as input—what tasks each employee performs in a day. The remedy, the path to greater productivity, is to focus on output.

Start with the customer—preferably, the taxpayer—although clearly some agencies will have only other agencies as customers. Let the customer define the desired results and the metrics that will be used to track them. Then focus on delivering those results in a fashion that meets or exceeds customer expectations. Keep pressing for ways to increase output, making the agency's deliverables better, faster, and, ultimately, cheaper. Finally, design incentives, such as pay bonuses, to let employees share in the efficiencies they create.

I am well aware that, under the current system, virtually none of these changes could be implemented by executive fiat. It will indeed take new and visionary legislation to clear a path for reform. But the opportunity is profound—not only for the federal government but also for the entire economy of our nation.

Viewed correctly, the chance to improve the performance of the federal workforce represents a "can't lose" proposition for public and private sectors alike. As you surely know, there are few such opportunities in the world. I sincerely hope you will see the value of this one and seize it. Perhaps, by breaking new ground and really giving some energy and attention to managing this responsibility, you may find the means to create in your tenure a legacy of unique and lasting value—an efficient high-performing federal government which draws upon the full potential of all of its employees.

ARCHIE W. DUNHAM

A rchie W. Dunham joined Conoco Inc. in 1966 and has served as president and chief executive officer of Conoco Inc., an integrated, international energy company, since 1996. In 1999 he was named chairman. Mr. Dunham formerly held the position of executive vice president. He was also a senior vice president for DuPont, Conoco's parent company at the time. Mr. Dunham holds a bachelor of science degree in geological engineering and a master of business administration degree from the University of Oklahoma.

Archie W. Dunham
Chairman,
President and
Chief Executive Officer

Conoco Inc.
P. O. Box 2197
Houston, TX 77252
(281) 293-1307

MEMORANDUM

TO: President-elect of the United States

FROM: Archie W. Dunham, Chairman, President,
             and Chief Executive Officer, Conoco Inc.

SUBJECT: Sustaining a Learning Culture

Congratulations on winning our nation's highest office; it's an honor to be invited to share my thoughts with you.

You have placed the subject of education high on your list of priorities, and I applaud this focus. As you know it's vital that America's children receive the finest education possible, if our nation is to thrive in a competitive world. Similarly, one of my major challenges as a leader of an energy company is to create a continuous learning culture within the corporate environment to ensure continuous growth in shareholder value and personal leadership. I believe the need for constant development of people in the private sector is paralleled in government. Just as shareholders greatly benefit when industry is led by empowered, enthusiastic, and efficient people, the citizens of a country have much to gain when those who administer government are equally empowered, enthusiastic, and efficient. The leaders of corporations have the responsibility to innovate through human and technological advances, as do U.S. government officials have the global responsibility to be models for efficient and caring administrations everywhere. How can this be accomplished?

I believe programs designed to establish sustainable development of human resources, just as we seek sustainable development of so many other resources, are crucial to the success of your goals. Along these lines, we have created a process at Conoco that is proving to be so popular and dynamic that I hope it can serve as a blueprint for establishing a similar plan for federal employees.

Like many large companies, we've established a corporate university to offer development opportunities to our 16,000 worldwide employees. The university's charge is to develop leadership skills and to advance fundamental skills, such as business literacy and personal development. The overall curriculum includes computer-based courses, as well as a generous mix of "classroom" experiences, often taught by our own senior officials.

Conoco's Trailblazer™: Advance Business Literacy, Personal Development

I want to focus on one of Conoco University's most important programs—an initiative specifically designed to train leaders who, over time, will create a new management model for Conoco. This new model supports our university's vision of sustaining a learning environment that is premier in the energy industry and beyond. We call this leadership program Trailblazer™. It was created through a unique collaboration among Conoco, London Business School, the Center for Creative Leadership, and JMW Consultants.

Management participants engage in development work
before, during, and after three intensive, one-week sessions that
occur over a nine-month period. An Intranet site bridges the
time between sessions with chat rooms, video presentations,
hyperlinks to applicable information, work-group sessions, and
reading assignments. Both the sessions and the available materials on the Web are important facets of the educational program.

Participants are carefully selected, based on their capacity
for aggressive development, their potential for holding a position of high-impact capability, and their promise as future business or functional executives. Because they come from our
global workforce, their diversity ensures that each "class" has
collectively been exposed to a mix of customer expectations,
alliance partners, service suppliers, governments, and host communities. As a result, graduates are provided an unusual opportunity to recognize emerging global business patterns.

Senior Officials Share Experiences and Meet the Company's Emerging Leaders

Each class involves approximately 25 employees, generally com-
prising senior managers, future leaders, and select employees
involved in major business initiatives. Faculty includes senior
management (including me—I greatly enjoy teaching these
bright young people) as well as world-renowned business
scholars and experts. Having our senior executives teach in
the program allows them to share their experience and also to
become better acquainted with the company's emerging leaders.

Participants select a critical business challenge to focus on
over the duration of the program. When these challenges are

shared and discussed, support networks automatically develop and new ideas are spawned. Also, a fair share of peer pressure kicks in, as each person strives to do well in front of colleagues. Consequently, by the end of the program, each person has a greater appreciation for the myriad of challenges faced by our global enterprise, as well as a better understanding of the company's direction and its collective leadership expertise.

The first session is held at London Business School. In a tightly compressed and intense week, participants build a shared understanding of current and future industry dynamics. Issues include global trends, competitive position, strategic architecture and core competence, implementation challenges, and corporate renewal opportunities. These new perspectives give each participant encouragement to address his or her own critical business challenge.

Evaluating Skills, Leveraging Knowledge, and Assuring Collaboration

The remaining two weeklong sessions are held in Houston, Conoco's worldwide headquarters. The second session focuses on the effectiveness of the individual, and is complemented by surveys completed by subordinates, peers, and supervisors that reveal strengths and weaknesses of the participant, and evaluate skill levels in areas such as conflict resolution and bringing out the best in people. Session three focuses on organization learning, elevating participants' ability to impact Conoco through sustained learning and collaboration, and synthesizes all the teachings of the program to help employees leverage knowledge and collaboration across and beyond the company.

Trailblazer™ is intended to transform Conoco beyond the the three-S approach (Strategy-Structure-Systems) to business that characterized twentieth-century thought to the three-P approach (Purpose-Process-People) that integrates business knowledge, personal effectiveness, and shared learning. Business experts recommend such an approach to develop a structure in which senior executives are the business system architects; regional or functional managers are the facilitators; and frontline managers or supervisors are the entrepreneurs.

Trailblazer™ is built on the traditional premise that effective strategies, structures, and systems will logically emerge from a program that taps the collective intelligence of everyone in the organization. The traditional foundation is intended to produce sustainability—through resilience. Success in achieving a sustainable leadership system will produce corporate growth and competitive advantage and open the door for the three-P approach.

Paying Attention to Human Values

To my knowledge, Trailblazer's™ curriculum is unlike anything else inside a corporate university or an academic institution, and I believe it gives Conoco a critical advantage. Business has changed. It is no longer enough to increase shareholder value through company growth. How the new goals are accomplished is of equal importance. I strongly believe the best companies pay the most attention to human values in the new world of work. I like the way business author Thomas Petzinger said it in his book, *The New Pioneers: The Men and Women Who Are Transforming the Workplace and Marketplace:*

In an era when change arrives without warning and threatens to eradicate the foundation of entire companies and entire industries overnight, organizations can survive only by becoming more human. Business that fails to engage the eyes, ears, minds and emotions of every individual in the organization will find themselves overrun by obsolescence or crushed by competition.

Trailblazer™ is in its early stages, and will be improved through experience. But early returns for the program are in. This e-mail came from a Norwegian participant, and his thoughts are similar to others who have attended: "Even though I used to be a very outspoken person before attending the Trailblazer™ program, I am even more to the point in my daily dealings with other people. My direct reports have given me feedback that we are making quicker decisions now as potential conflicts and differences of opinion are brought to the table faster. Personally, I feel this has been a great experience, as I spend less time worrying about what might go wrong and rather try to look for what is possible when potential conflicts occur."

Attracting, Retaining, and Challenging Outstanding People

Mr. President-elect, I firmly believe that investment in the development of people is a defining factor of success. Attracting and retaining outstanding people and challenging them to develop to their full potential is a critical necessity of both industry and government. We implemented Trailblazer™ in an environment of flux when oil prices were low and when all investments were undergoing severe scrutiny. I firmly believe it was the right decision, because it is primarily our people, not the ever-changing business environment that will determine Conoco's long-term success. I hope this description of our experiment in learning is valuable to you and your administration.

INVESTMENT IN THE DEVELOPMENT OF PEOPLE IS A DEFINING FACTOR OF SUCCESS. ATTRACTING AND RETAINING OUTSTANDING PEOPLE AND CHALLENGING THEM TO DEVELOP TO THEIR FULL POTENTIAL IS A CRITICAL NECESSITY OF BOTH INDUSTRY AND GOVERNMENT.

My best wishes for your personal success as president, and for the success of the United States of America.

CHARLES M. BREWER

Charles M. Brewer founded Mind-Spring Enterprises, Inc., in 1994, and is chairman of EarthLink, Inc. He previously served as chief executive officer for AudioFax, Inc., a software company, and was vice president of Sanders & Company, a venture capital firm. Mr. Brewer holds a bachelor's degree in economics from Amherst College and a master of business administration degree from Stanford University.

EARTHLINK | 1430 W. Peachtree Street NW
Suite 400
Atlanta, GA 30309
Phone 404.815.0770
Fax 404.815.8805

EarthLink

MEMORANDUM

TO: President-elect of the United States

FROM: Charles M. Brewer, Founder, MindSpring
             Enterprises, Inc., and Chairman, EarthLink, Inc.

SUBJECT: Leading with Values

Lead by establishing the values and principles that will drive
the daily actions of each and every government employee. Make
this your highest priority. Do it authentically, consistently, and
passionately. If you do, you will make government service a calling that once again attracts the brightest and noblest of our citizens, reestablish the confidence of the American people in their
government, and accomplish great things.

Let me explain why I believe this is true.

The Nature of People and Work

I believe that nearly all people want to accomplish something
really great with their work. They want to go home at the end
of the day feeling proud of what they have accomplished. They
are willing to make sacrifices and exert great efforts to make
this happen. These are normal human traits—not something
possessed only by an extraordinary few.

An Unfortunate Tendency of Organizations

Yet when these well-intentioned individuals gather together into organizations, something insidious can happen. Most of them end up feeling that they are not doing a great job, not accomplishing anything very worthwhile, and that there is something about the way their organization functions that makes it nearly impossible for them to do so. As a result, many people eventually give up on getting satisfaction and feelings of accomplishment from their work. They can't quit, because they need the paycheck, but at some point they decide that they will just have to get their satisfaction from something else—like their hobbies or their children. For the years or decades that remain in their working careers, work delivers nothing but a paycheck. What they provide to their organizations is in turn equally meager—a mere fraction of what they could contribute.

How Can an Organization Help Individuals Reach Their Goals?

For years I became increasingly frustrated and discouraged by this state of affairs, but I just didn't know what to do about it. After all, nobody has ever intentionally created a company or an organization thinking, "I'm going to make this a place where nobody can ever do good work or feel proud about it." It happens in spite of good intentions, not because of bad intentions. So if one wants to create an organization that is somehow different and better than this depressing status quo, where would he or she start? It can't be just picking the people for the organization. They will come and go over time, and if I'm right about the basic nature of people it is not the individuals who are the problem anyway. And it can't be picking the product or the line of business for the organization—that too will change over time as market forces dictate. So what is the answer?

I think there is only one possibility. If you want to create an organization that really is dramatically different and better, the key to success is to focus on the values and philosophy that drive the organization. By doing so you can create an organization where people are able to do what they already want to do— accomplish something really worthwhile and go home at the end of the day feeling proud about it. The impact of this is huge—not only for the individuals, but also for the organization. You end up with people who are not just a little bit more productive than employees in a typical setting, but really dramatically so. And that, of course, makes it easy for the organization to serve its customers and its owners extraordinarily well.

A Real-World Example

When I set out to start a company in the spring of 1993, I didn't know what the company would do, but I had some very firm ideas about what it would be like—how we would treat each other, and how we would treat our customers. I desperately wanted us to be different than the depressing status quo, and I thought that the key to doing so would be to make the values of the company our primary focus and foundation. We call them our Core Values and Beliefs, or CV&Bs. Here they are—unchanged since the beginning except for the subsequent addition of number five.

1. We respect the individual, and believe that individuals who are treated with respect and given responsibility respond by giving their best.

2. We require complete honesty and integrity in everything we do.

3. We make commitments with care, and then live up to them. In all things, we do what we say we are going to do.

4. Work is an important part of life, and it should be fun. Being a good businessperson does not mean being stuffy and boring.

5. We love to compete, and we believe that competition brings out the best in us.

6. We are frugal. We guard and conserve the company's resources with at least the same vigilance that we would use to guard and conserve our own personal resources.

7. We insist on giving our best effort in everything we undertake. Furthermore, we see a huge difference between "good mistakes" (best effort, bad result) and "bad mistakes" (sloppiness or lack of effort).

8. Clarity in understanding our mission, our goals, and what we expect from each other is critical to our success.

9. We are believers in the Golden Rule ("do to others as you would have them do to you"). In all our dealings we will strive to be friendly and courteous, as well as fair and compassionate.

10. We feel a sense of urgency on any matters related to our customers. We own problems and we are always responsive. We are customer-driven.

You might say that our foundation is one of respect for the individual and honesty. We try to create an environment where we let people do great work rather than try to make them do great work.

THE MOST IMPORTANT REASON FOR PEOPLE
TO COME WORK [AT EARTHLINK] HAS
ALWAYS BEEN BECAUSE THEY ARE REALLY
EXCITED ABOUT OUR VISION OF BUILDING A
DIFFERENT AND BETTER KIND OF COMPANY.
AND BY THE WAY, NOT EVERYONE GETS
EXCITED ABOUT THAT. SOME PEOPLE THINK
THE WHOLE THING SOUNDS HOKEY AND
NAÏVE AND THAT WE ARE DOOMED TO FAIL
IN THE REAL WORLD WHERE YOU NEED TO
LIE, CHEAT, AND STEAL TO GET AHEAD. WE
DON'T HIRE THOSE PEOPLE.

By early 1994, I finally decided that the line of business for this new company would be as an Internet Service Provider (ISP), and I named it MindSpring. There was nothing particularly unique about that. We started around the same time as literally thousands of other local ISPs. We had a technically inept founder (me), not much money, no proprietary technology, no proprietary marketing advantage, no proprietary anything except for our vision of the values that would drive how we'd treat each other and how we'd treat our customers.

The most important reason for people to come work here has always been because they are really excited about our vision of building a different and better kind of company. And by the way, not everyone gets excited about that. Some people think the whole thing sounds hokey and naïve and that we are doomed to fail in the real world where you need to lie, cheat, and steal to get ahead. We don't hire those people. And since the beginning, we have tried to make our decisions in the context of the CV&Bs. For example, at many times in our early history we were unable to get new dial-in phone-line capacity as rapidly as we needed it. When that happened our response was to think about CV&B number three, "making commitments with care and living up to them." With that as a guide it was obvious to us that the right decision was to not take any new customers onto the system until we could get the new phone lines to handle them. It seems obvious, but competitors without a firm values foundation—from the smallest ones to the largest ones—almost never made that choice.

In the early days of our business, we had, objectively speaking, a pitiful infrastructure. Our network hub was located in the basement of a suburban house. Our modems, all eight of them, came from the local computer store. Our servers were two 486 computers. And as you'd expect, our service was not that reliable. The modems would lock up, the phone lines would malfunction, etc., etc. Yet somehow, even then, our customers loved us. They could tell that first of all, we were telling them the truth—no matter how embarrassing. This was in marked contrast to many other ISPs who would never, ever, admit that they were anything but perfect. Second, customers could tell that we were doing our absolute best to do the right thing for them—even if in the short term it appeared to be the wrong thing for the company. And third, they came to believe that we were probably at least as competent as the next guys. As a result, customers liked us! Or more accurately, they liked how we treated them. And because of that, we quickly became the leading ISP in our local market, growing to 1,000 customers by the end of 1994. From there we have continued to grow from thousands of customers, to tens of thousands, to hundreds of thousands, to millions.

Lots of people, even some great admirers of the company in its early stages, doubted whether our values and culture could survive growth. But, the values-based approach and the culture that comes with it has survived. I think I know why. If the values commitment is driven by just one or a few leaders of the company, then as the company grows the values will become more and more diluted until eventually they have no influence at all. In other words, they won't scale. If, on the other hand, the values leadership really comes from everybody, then the more you grow the more values leaders you have, and it scales to infinity. And I think that is really what happened with us. The new people joining the company are so fresh and enthusiastic that they keep the rest of us pumped up.

Anyhow, we have certainly been dramatically more successful than most ISPs. We rank number one in industry customer-satisfaction surveys with remarkable regularity. We have grown from local to regional to national, and now, following the Mind-

Spring/EarthLink merger, we are the second-largest ISP in the country with over 3.5 million customers and about 7,000 employees. I don't know what else to blame this success on other than our values-based approach to the business, and the thousands of everyday triumphs of people who feel that they've found a place where they can be themselves, give their best, and feel proud about it.

What Are the Keys to Making Values-Based Management Work?

First, it has to be absolutely authentic. If the leaders don't deeply believe in the values that they promote, or if they don't provide credible role models of living up to them, the chances of success with this are zero. People are too smart. They will know. They have a sixth sense for this.

Beyond that, the steps to creating a values-based organization are: articulate the values, select people who fit the values, and build the values into the structure of the organization.

Articulating the values means talking about them, writing about them, making them a part of your day-to-day conversation and activities.

Selecting the right people means that the number-one criterion for hiring is an excellent fit with the values. You can certainly look for evidence in candidates' backgrounds to tell you how well they fit. Also, just ask them! If they can't convincingly explain why they are enthusiastic about the mission to build your values-based organization, you'll be able to tell. You have the same built-in sixth sense that everyone else does in sensing that authenticity!

Selecting the right people also means that people who get pro-
moted in the organization will be the best values role models
and the best values leaders. Of course, it also means people who
don't fit the values have to leave—no doubt about it!

Building the values into the structure of the organization
means that the metrics, systems, and processes that support the
organization will support the values and not work against them.
For example, if "always being responsive to our customers" is a
value you seek to promote, you'll certainly have to invest in systems to increase and measure responsiveness. If one of the
values is "we believe that individuals who are treated with
respect and given responsibility respond by giving their best"
then you'll certainly create management structures that give
individual employees wide latitude in how they accomplish
their work assignments.

Does This Apply to Government?

Oh yes! Even more so than in business. Even now, idealists
often to want to serve in government. The essence of government service should be to strive to make a difference, to accomplish something to be proud of. On the other hand, the profit
motivation that drives some portion of behavior in the business
world is not present in government work. And in government
there are generally no market forces to weed out poor performers. A values framework and leadership that supports people in
striving for accomplishments, and one that provides the discipline to weed out mediocrity, is even more critical here than in
business.

Some Values to Consider

If you are to succeed with a values-based approach to building government, you'll need to use values that are authentically yours. Maybe some of ours will inspire you, but I believe some different emphasis is needed in a government setting. Here are two that I'd love to see on your list.

- Our highest responsibility is to uphold the honesty, integrity, and fairness of the United States government at all times.

  My reason for this one is that I think our government has historically been too quick to engage in pragmatic, unprincipled, or "realpolitik" thinking. The ends justify the means. I think it is a huge mistake. Our country's founding principles are our greatest strength. Let that shine forth with full integrity! This will be hugely important to attracting the really great people and supercharging their accomplishments.
- The citizens of this country are our customers and our owners. We will not tolerate mediocrity in serving them.

We require best efforts and superlative performance from our colleagues and ourselves. As we have all seen too often, government tends to treat us citizens like its subjects. That's backwards! We are the customers! We deserve the best service, not the worst! And guess what—most of the government employees providing that lousy service know it is lousy, and they don't like it either. They aren't proud of giving lousy service! They want to accomplish something they can be proud of! Root out the mediocrity, and exterminate it. Does this mean some people will have to be fired? Absolutely. But the ones who remain, and the new ones who join, will perform better than you might dare dream.

You have over two million employees. It will be impossible for you to know the first thing about most of their jobs. But you can be confident that the large majority of them want to do great work. They want to accomplish something meaningful. Your leadership in setting the values for the organization can be the key to letting them succeed.

FRED HASSAN

Fred Hassan is president and chief executive officer of Pharmacia Corporation, created in 2000 after the merger of Pharmacia & Upjohn and Monsanto Company. Previously, he was executive vice president of American Home Products, headed Genetics Institute, Inc., and spent 17 years with Sandoz Pharmaceutical Corporation (now Novartis). Mr. Hassan holds a bachelor's degree from the Imperial College of Science and Technology at the University of London and a master of business administration degree from Harvard Business School.

Pharmacia Corporation
100 Route 206 North
Peapack, New Jersey 07977
(908) 901-8895
Fax (908) 901-1805

FRED HASSAN
Chief Executive Officer

PHARMACIA

MEMORANDUM

TO: President-elect of the United States

FROM: Fred Hassan, President and Chief Executive
            Officer, Pharmacia Corporation

SUBJECT: Changing Results by Changing Behaviors

Just like the United States has the vision to be a "best-governed country," Pharmacia has set itself a vision of being the "best-managed company" in its own industry. Being big, by itself, does not bring greatness. But being best managed can lead to greatness—in governments, just as in companies.

In government, as in business, there is often a preoccupation with organizational structure. Get the structure right, so the thinking goes, and a more efficient operation will follow.

There's no question that having an organizational structure that matches the strategy is important. However, as both private sector and public sector organizations become far more complex, a focus on structure can obscure what is becoming a far more critical factor in management success: effective management *behaviors*.

Horizontal work processes, well executed, will differentiate the successful companies from the also rans in the twenty-first century—just like the twentieth century ushered in the era of scientific management that emphasized division of labor, vertical specialist functions, and sophisticated organization charts.

In fact, as we are finding in our own fast-changing global company, instilling effective management behaviors is a way of overcoming the barriers and silos that naturally result from organizational structures, however sophisticated. This is because no single organizational structure today can respond to the very fast changing global environment, or to the increasingly complex demands of customers—who, for you, Mr. President-elect, will be every American citizen.

We are also finding that a common set of well-understood core behaviors for managers creates unity and direction across the organization, integrating different locations, business units, and cultures.

However, the kinds of behaviors that we are demanding of our managers are not easy to instill, because many of them run counter to territorial human instincts. So we've also devoted a great deal of time and effort to rewarding the right behaviors among managers—assuring, in other words, that what we *say* in this critical area is what our people also *do*.

At Pharmacia, we have distilled our behavioral code into five simple, but, I believe, profound directions for our managers. These five points apply to managers in every part of our very diverse business, from managers in charge of production workers in our global supply operations in the United States and Europe to R&D managers directing our highly talented and individualistic research scientists, and to country presidents responsible for our commercial operations in dozens of locations worldwide.

We call these five points the Pharmacia "Best-Managed" behaviors. This code reflects our commitment to becoming the best-managed company in our global industry—because by being best managed we will become best at serving our customers and patients, which in turn will generate industry best performance. I believe that the implementation of these same five core behaviors can dramatically improve the functioning of our government organizations—because "best-managed" in that context is no less than "best-governed."

1. Shared Accountability and Transparency

Most organizations today focus strongly on accountability—but mainly, it is accountability of individuals or of specific units for meeting their goals. In increasingly complex and fast-changing environments, however, it is not enough for individuals or single business areas to be responsible for "rowing their own individual boats"—because company results are usually a function of different people in different departments relying on the results of others for their own success.

For this reason, we are building a management behavior of *shared* accountability. The message to all our managers is that to a large extent, their success is collective and interdependent. Managers need to be responsible *collectively*. By creating an atmosphere and expectation of shared accountability, we move the instinctive process from "I" to "we," and from individual or department results to the total organization's satisfaction of cus-

tomer needs. This of course also requires setting broader performance goals. Success for an R&D unit, for example, must be
defined not simply in terms of the number of new compounds
it files for approval, but instead in terms of the relevance of the
group's discovery and development to key areas of medical
need and to the commercial results in the marketplace.

MANAGERS NEED TO BE RESPONSIBLE
COLLECTIVELY. BY CREATING AN
ATMOSPHERE AND EXPECTATION OF SHARED
ACCOUNTABILITY, WE MOVE THE
INSTINCTIVE PROCESS FROM "I" TO "WE,"
AND FROM INDIVIDUAL OR DEPARTMENT
RESULTS TO THE TOTAL ORGANIZATION'S
SATISFACTION OF CUSTOMER NEEDS.

With shared accountability for results goes *transparency*. It's
amazing how secretive individual work units can be about such
basics as budgets and management decision making. However,
as behaviors that result from shared accountability take hold, it
is the managers themselves who begin to demand transparency
from each other. They reasonably begin to expect that if they
are to be held accountable for the total results of the organization, they also have the right and responsibility to influence
decisions in units outside their direct management areas. And of
course, the additional sunlight, coupled with peer review, in the
end improves everyone's processes and enhances overall results.

2. Participative Management

Participative management is closely tied to shared accountability for results. Like shared accountability, it goes against some of our most basic human, territorial urges. But like shared accountability, participative management offers a step change in organizational effectiveness.

> TEAMWORK HAS BECOME A BUZZWORD IN THE WORKPLACE TODAY. . . . THE GREAT CHALLENGE FOR THIS NEW CENTURY WILL BE TEAMWORK *BETWEEN* WORK GROUPS. MORE AND MORE, THE MANAGEMENT CHALLENGE FOR ALL COMPLEX ORGANIZATIONS WILL LIE IN CREATING A SEAMLESS FLOW OF EFFECTIVE ACTIONS ACROSS A SERIES OF BUSINESS UNITS.

Participative management—in contrast to the traditional command and control management—seeks to bridge the gap between those who direct and those who execute so that there is a fuller involvement, and commitment and shared ownership for the task at hand.

As we all know, teamwork has become a buzzword in the workplace today. Yet while most organizations have made a lot of progress in achieving teamwork within individual work groups, the great challenge for this new century will be teamwork *between* work groups. More and more, the management challenge for all complex organizations will lie in creating a seamless flow of effective actions across a series of business units.

In the pharmaceutical industry, this is illustrated by the drug development process, from early discovery of new compounds to the delivery of new treatments to patients. Often it takes 15 years from the start of the project to the delivery of the drug to the patient. Each project needs innovation, speed, and flexibility to adjust to changing assumptions. Each area of responsibility along the chain—research, development, manufacturing, marketing, and sales—can be doing excellent work in its own silo, and yet the result can be suboptimal—because as each silo tosses the project on to the next, knowledge, value, and efficiency may be lost.

The concept of participative management is aimed directly at overcoming this challenge. The key is cross-functional teamwork. We make it part of our managers' job descriptions to create team relationships with the various units "before" them and "after" them in the product flow chain. We also set the clear expectation that their *people* will demonstrate the same behavior. The way we put it is "be exquisitely good at your functional role within your unit—but achieve your goal by collaborating outside your unit."

What's interesting—and also productive—about this new behavior is that the relationship between managers and their reports changes dramatically. The top-down, hierarchical management style disintegrates because employees are liberated to work and formulate decisions outside their formal reporting structure, as part of cross-functional teams.

The benefits of participative management are quantifiable and striking. One of the most critical success factors in the pharmaceutical industry is the minimization of time from the discovery of an innovative new medication to the submission of its complete data package to regulatory authorities. Several years ago, we consciously implemented participative management behaviors in the units across the company that were working on a revolutionary new antibiotic called Zyvox. Late last year we filed Zyvox with the FDA: 4.9 years from first dose in man to market, with the industry median at 6.8 years. It is already making an enormous difference to thousands of patients who have access to a life-saving treatment earlier than anyone had thought possible.

3. Continuous Improvement against Benchmarks

Most managers set goals against internal budgets and standards. That's normal and necessary to some degree—but it's not a good way to keep up with competitors, who may be setting higher goals, or with customers, who may be setting higher standards.

As part of our "best-managed" behaviors package, we are training our managers to set their performance goals against *external* benchmarks defined by two critical groups: our competitors and our customers.

In our field force, for example, we've focused our district managers on benchmarking the number of calls on doctors and products discussed per call compared to what our top competitor's medical representatives accomplish per day—a key measure of productivity. We have also taken independent surveys that tell us how the doctors, and especially the high-volume doctors, rate the quality of our representatives' calls versus those top-performing competitors. Sometimes what we learned was discomforting, but it has forcefully fostered new thinking and new actions. We are seeing concrete results: steady improvement by our teams against the benchmarks and steady improvement in the utilization of our products.

4. Listening and Learning

I tell our managers regularly that I learn as much on the job each day as I did each day in business school. That learning comes through effective listening to others. Dynamic listening and learning is probably the single most important component of success in my CEO role.

ONCE THESE LISTENING AND LEARNING BEHAVIORS START TO BE ADOPTED BY MANAGERS, WE SEE THEM SPREAD TO OTHER EMPLOYEES. THEY TOO BEGIN LISTENING AND LEARNING WITH EACH OTHER—AND WITH CUSTOMERS. A GREAT SIDE EFFECT IS INCREASED MUTUAL RESPECT AND TRUST. OUR MANAGERS BEGIN TO REGARD THEIR WORK TEAM AS A SOURCE OF KNOWLEDGE, NOT JUST A MEANS OF EXECUTING THEIR COMMANDS.

For example, one of my most important sources of listening and learning is my regular meetings with small groups of employees at the grassroots, where I ask for advice on how I can do my job better.

Yet most managers are deficient in both these areas—partly due to time pressures and partly due to learned behaviors of command and control.

We focus on building listening and learning behavior in managers both internally, to our own people and each other, and externally, to the competitive environment and our customers.

With a few exceptions, effective listening and learning in a managerial role does not come naturally to people. They are skills that need to be learned. "Active" listening in particular is a skill that comes through coaching and practice. Getting employees, colleagues, or customers to say what they *really* think and properly understanding what they said calls for active listening techniques that include an understanding of behavioral psychology.

Once these listening and learning behaviors start to be adopted by managers, we see them spread to other employees. They too begin listening and learning with each other—and with customers. A great side effect is increased mutual respect and trust. Our managers begin to regard their work team as a source of knowledge, not just a means of executing their commands. And our people begin to feel comfortable giving feedback and recommendations to management. Our company consistently becomes smarter. Everyone benefits—especially our customers.

5. Coaching

The last of our five "best-managed" behaviors is coaching and developing other employees.

Coaching is different from the more widespread concept of mentoring. Mentoring is a great idea, but it is a top-down process from mentor to mentoree.

Coaching, by contrast, can and should take place in all directions: from above, from peers, and even from subordinates.

Across our organization, we encourage different responsibility areas to be coaches to each other. For example, in cross-functional meetings and one-on-one interactions, our commercial people coach their research and development colleagues on the customer behavior aspects of our business—and vice versa.

A very important factor in building a coaching environment is also building a receptivity to coaching among the people—especially, receptivity to being coached by peers and even subordinates in the organization. One needs managers to feel very secure and comfortable and to understand the coaching concept as a 360-degree approach to improvement.

Changing behaviors in an organization is perhaps the most profound change you can undertake. So to implement our best-managed behaviors package we have recognized that we need to place these desired behaviors very high on the radar screen of our people and to back them up with major incentives.

So we've done just that. We ask all of our senior managers to incorporate these behaviors in some form into their own personal objectives for each year. To send the right signal, implementing these behaviors is one of my own five personal objectives as CEO.

We are also using our incentive program to dramatically reinforce this priority. Around 30 percent of our top management group's variable compensation is tied to their commitment to, and practice of, the five best-managed behaviors at Pharmacia.

The need to have consistent incentives is one of the most important lessons I have learned. To implement best-managed behaviors one is asking people to operate in ways that initially can be very uncomfortable and threatening. One needs to convey very strongly the message that "we are serious about this," combined with the message that "in the end, the individuals will benefit, and so will the organization." It's hard work, but I know it's been worth it for us. I am sure it can work for you as you set about the task of building a best-managed government and a best-governed country.

JOSEPH D. SARGENT

Joseph D. Sargent is president and chief
executive officer of The Guardian Life
Insurance Company of America. He
joined the company in 1959 upon graduation
from Fairfield University. A frequent industry
speaker, Mr. Sargent also contributes often to
insurance industry publications. Mr. Sargent
has received the Ellis Island Medal of Freedom and Fairfield University's Professional
Achievement Award.

GUARDIAN

Joseph D. Sargent, CLU
President
and Chief Executive Officer

MEMORANDUM

TO: The President-elect of the United States

FROM: Joseph D. Sargent, President and Chief Executive Officer, The Guardian Life Insurance Company of America

SUBJECT: Promoting Ethical Behavior in Large Organizations

Let me begin by offering my congratulations and best wishes for your tenure as leader of our great country. Though the task that faces you as our new president has many challenges, there are also wonderful opportunities to make a real difference in the lives of millions.

I remember reading a quote from the CEO of another firm saying, in effect, that when he became the head of his company he became the servant of all the people who worked in that company. When you take over the presidency in a few months, you too will have to think of your position in those terms, because in a democracy you can't tell people what to think, feel, or do. Yet in doing their work, you can have a powerful influence on their behavior. To paraphrase Dwight D. Eisenhower, leadership is getting other people to do what you want them to do because *they* want to do it.

It was quite a challenge for me to select a topic to discuss with you for this book. After some deliberation, I decided to share my perspective on a subject I have given a great deal of thought to, as a CEO of a major corporation with thousands of employees nationwide: the ways in which a leader can promote ethical behavior. I think it's crucial that you convey the need for the highest ethical standards and behavior possible to your new appointees and the civil service. In addition, I think I can bring an interesting perspective to the subject since ethics is the cornerstone of how my own industry operates.

When you are selling an intangible product like life insurance, you are essentially selling a promise that 20, 30, 50 or more years down the road, the product will perform as expected—and you will be there to fulfill the obligation. When people give you their hard-earned money based on a promise you've made, you have not only a fiduciary responsibility but also an enormous moral responsibility. Our business is built on that responsibility, and succeeds or fails on our commitment to meeting it.

Speaking personally, I have been fortunate: more than 40 years ago I joined Guardian—a company that had an extremely strong tradition of ethical behavior and a culture to match. The tradition was begun even before our actual start of business in 1860, when Guardian's founder Hugo Wesendonck raised twice the capital required to begin an insurance company. Simply "following the rules" would have been much more expeditious and perfectly acceptable. But Wesendonck believed the required amount was not a sufficient guarantee of the ability to pay claims and dividends, and therefore not in the best interests of policyowners. Thus Guardian began with this quite simple and yet profound moral lesson: adhering strictly to the letter of the law is not the same as behaving ethically.

This culture was so ingrained at our company that at the beginning of the last century, when Congress was conducting its Armstrong investigations of the insurance business and thus setting off a wave of reform in our industry, Guardian was specifically commended for its ethics and concern for the customer.

Another incident a few decades later clearly demonstrates these ethical standards at work. Branch Rickey, general manager of the Brooklyn Dodgers, was also a member of Guardian's board of directors. When the Dodgers signed Jackie Robinson, Rickey submitted his resignation to the board. Integration was controversial in 1947, and Rickey didn't want the company to become a target in the conflict. When his resignation was read to the board, everything was quiet for a moment. Then a board member named F. W. Lafrentz spoke. "I move we table Mr. Rickey's resignation," he said. "And more power to Mr. Rickey."

There was, of course, no video camera running. No squadrons of PR people phoning the story to the newspapers. No polls taken before or after to find out how the decision would play with the public. It was simply the right thing to do.

When I came to Guardian fresh out of college, I was told that we in the home office had one overriding responsibility day in and day out: to do the right thing for all—our agents, our policyowners, and our employees. Naturally, as CEO, I still feel it's my daily responsibility. I hope you agree that as president you will have a similar duty to do the right thing on behalf of your constituents. And you will have, as any leader does, expe-

riences in which your ability to carry out that responsibility will
be tested.

Enforcing Ethics

For example, there was an incident in which one of our agents
was found to have been involved in knowingly inappropriate
behavior in placing business with the company. The agent concerned was a long-time friend of mine. While I was advised to
invoke some minimal censure, I had to follow what I believed
and I felt termination was necessary. The organization needed
to know that everyone, regardless of position or personal relationship, would be held to the same standard of behavior.

A leader cannot merely say "I didn't authorize it" while turning a blind eye to his subordinates' actions. I have found that the
beliefs and behavior of the leader and his team quickly filter
through an organization. If it's known that unethical behavior
will not be tolerated, the general tone of organizational behavior
will be lifted. People generally want to act ethically and welcome
the confirmation that their leaders do so as well.

Aside from personal issues, doing the right thing can sometimes put you at odds with your peers. We made news throughout our industry in the 1980s, when many companies were rapidly developing new products to take advantage of short-term
economic conditions. In spite of some advice to the contrary, we
decided not to push ahead with the development of one particular product because we were not satisfied it was in the best
interest of the policyowner. It was particularly gratifying to me
that when I shared this with our field force, there was unan-
imous acceptance of the decision. Some companies did offer

this product and more than a few attempted to modify it and "dress it up" to make it more acceptable. But as my predecessor Leo Futia used to say, "There is no right way to do a wrong thing."

A LEADER CANNOT MERELY SAY "I DIDN'T AUTHORIZE IT" WHILE TURNING A BLIND EYE TO HIS SUBORDINATES' ACTIONS. I HAVE FOUND THAT THE BELIEFS AND BEHAVIOR OF THE LEADER AND HIS TEAM QUICKLY FILTER THROUGH AN ORGANIZATION. IF IT'S KNOWN THAT UNETHICAL BEHAVIOR WILL NOT BE TOLERATED, THE GENERAL TONE OF THE ORGANIZATIONAL BEHAVIOR WILL BE LIFTED. PEOPLE GENERALLY WANT TO ACT ETHICALLY AND WELCOME THE CONFIRMA-TION THAT THEIR LEADERS DO SO AS WELL.

Unfortunately, the competitive pressures of the 1980s did lead some financial services companies to adopt questionable sales practices and other abuses, which ultimately led to a rash of regulatory investigations and a wave of litigation. A company such as ours, with a mutual form of ownership (as opposed to stock ownership), has a special responsibility to protect its poli-cyholders' interests. During those times of cutthroat competition, our company clung to its belief that our policyowners were of primary concern. In the end, we not only survived, but prospered—which proves again, I think, that the right way ultimately proves the best way, whether in business or public affairs.

Building an Ethical Culture

In the wake of the public's increasing concern about ethical issues, many companies have issued rules of conduct, set up or strengthened legal compliance departments, and educated employees about integrity. This is necessary: values and ethics, after all, are much more than something to aspire to—they need to be clearly articulated and to be woven into the fabric of the culture. But while setting up corporate systems to ensure discipline is a necessary and worthwhile endeavor, these systems and rules don't in themselves create an ethical culture. In fact, they can increase cynicism if they're seen by employees and customers as an attempt to meet the letter of the law and thus help the company escape liability. Moral behavior is not a matter of following rules; it's about correctly aligning your internal compass. In an organization, it should be less about avoiding punishment and more about having a set of shared values and guiding principles.

In reexamining our own core values recently, we tried not to craft a set of ideals, but to identify the principles that seem to underlie our culture as it exists. We found that three key things make us all proud to work at Guardian: we do the right thing, people count at our company, and we hold ourselves to very high standards. In sharing these values with our employees, we are not asking them to do something new or telling them something they don't know already. We are simply articulating a culture that is already in place.

In the case of the federal government, there is an honorable tradition of public service on which to build. Both your political appointees and your career civil servants follow in a long line of distinguished public officials. It was one of them, the late Elliot Richardson, who wrote, "Public service is a public trust. The highest obligation of every individual in government is to fulfill that trust. Each person who undertakes the public trust makes two paramount commitments: to serve the public interest, and to perform with integrity."

Do as I Say *and as I Do*

There is no question that a leader of any organization, whether it's a company or a country, has a moral responsibility to "walk the talk." None of us can assume the responsibilities of leadership without recognizing that people watch our behavior in both public and private and assume that it will be consistent. People don't make a distinction between you as an individual and your role, for the simple reason that you as an individual have taken on the role. If you act improperly, people will know the ethics you promote don't mean that much to you.

It seems we live in a skeptical age. There will be those who question your sincerity, your motives, and your morality no matter what you do. Promoting ethical behavior and attempting to exemplify it are not a cure for cynicism. They are, however, a very effective answer to it.

I hope some of these thoughts are helpful as you begin to lead us into the bright future I believe we all share. Again, congratulations and best wishes as you take on your new role.

4

LEVERAGING
TECHNOLOGY

ESTHER DYSON

E sther Dyson is chairman of EDventure Holdings Inc., which publishes the influential computer-industry newsletter *Release 1.0* and sponsors two of the industry's premier conferences, PC Forum (U.S.) and EDventure High-Tech Forum (Europe). Ms. Dyson is an active investor in a variety of IT and Internet start-ups, in the United States and throughout Europe. She is a graduate of Harvard University.

EDVENTURE HOLDINGS INC.

Publisher of RELEASE 1.0
Sponsor of PC Forum & High-Tech Forum

M E M O R A N D U M

TO: President-elect of the United States

FROM: Esther Dyson, Chairman, EDventure Holdings Inc.

SUBJECT: Internet Privacy and Security Issues You Face

As the next U.S. president, what should you think and do about the Net?

You should indeed think—and understand—first. Few politicians actually understand the Net, though almost all now acknowledge its importance. They see it as a gift that the "haves" have and that the "have-nots" *should* have, or perhaps as a useful tool for government efficiency. But in fact, it is also a disruptive force, one that could upset the balance of power. As president, you will be, like it or not, the Establishment. The Net is profoundly anti-Establishment. It allows people to talk back. Worse, from the Establishment's point of view, the Net lets people bypass it. They can talk to each other without going through established channels. In short, the mass media are a great medium for you, and (let's face it) for propaganda. The Internet, by contrast, is a great medium for conspiracy. That's helpful in countries where the government needs truth telling or even toppling, but for you, it will be a challenge.

104 FIFTH AVENUE, 20TH FLOOR
NEW YORK, NY 10011-6987
1(212) 924-8800 FAX 1(212) 924-0240
WWW.EDVENTURE.COM

People will use the Net to challenge your authority, to spread lies, and to reveal uncomfortable truths. It will be harder and harder for you to simply say, "your government knows best."

A second thing to understand is how the Net changes your own role. More and more of what people do in the future will be beyond government control, de facto. For on-line services, from gambling to accounting services, the United States will be competing with other nations. So far, the United States has done pretty well in such competition. For example, many investors prefer to invest in the United States—not only in U.S. companies, but also under U.S. securities laws. Investors like the U.S. emphasis on clean accounting and disclosure. And companies seeking funds also come to U.S. markets to reach those investors, usually at prices higher than they could get in less-regulated markets. But in other areas, if you overregulate, you will find e-businesses fleeing the United States.

So, on the one hand, you have less control. On the other, you are in some sense the world's leader for Internet policies, since many governments (though not necessarily their citizens) will look to you and the United States for guidance in setting their own policies. The U.S. president rules the United States, but also leads the world, especially vis-à-vis the Net. Our influence isn't always appreciated, but it *is* acknowledged.

It is important that you think of the world at large, and not just the United States, when you consider Net policies. Not all governments are as benign as the United States, so policies that give the government the right to monitor conversations, restrict the use of encryption and require identification, may be imposed by other governments who are likely to abuse them. (And let's admit, as history shows, that not every individual in the U.S. government has been immune to the seductions of power.)

Thus, most of what you should do vis-à-vis the Net is show restraint. In the United States at least, the Internet is growing nicely of its own accord, supporting private communities, commercial ventures, political speech and discussion, and of course a broad diversity of news, opinion, and entertainment. All you need to do is avoid imposing too much control (do not attempt to regulate content! Let parents monitor their kids!), while at the same time fostering a Net that is robust and secure.

What follows are specific challenges in the areas of privacy and security.

Let the Infrastructure Flourish, and Keep It Fair

In the United States, unlike some other countries, the infrastructure is healthy, widespread, and growing healthily. Your major task here is to make sure that it remains open and competitive—that no single vendor gains too much power, that the cable companies or wireless networks don't restrict users' access to the full extent of the Web. Basically, you should support the FCC as it fosters competition, and you should make sure anti-trust laws are enforced. But you should also try not to meddle— just as the FCC has tried to let the open-access cable issue sort itself out. Your goal should be constraint of power, whether government power or business power.

Foster Security and Privacy

This is probably the most important challenge you will face. Security and privacy are two parts of the same issue.

E-commerce will blossom now only if people feel secure, and the important commercial, social, and political platform the Net offers will continue to flourish only if it *is* secure.

SECURITY IS LIKE PUBLIC HEALTH: INDIVIDUALS CAN ONLY DO SO MUCH TO PROTECT THEMSELVES. IT ALSO DEPENDS ON THE PEOPLE AROUND THEM. HOW CAN YOU, AS PRESIDENT, GET EVERYONE TO RISE TO THE CHALLENGE?

But you can't create security by law, nor can individuals achieve security for themselves. Security is like public health: Individuals can do only so much to protect themselves. It also depends on the people around them. How can you, as president, get everyone to rise to the challenge?

Unfortunately, the American public is sometimes pretty careless. If you ask people in a survey, they will tell you that privacy and security are important, but if you watch their *behavior* you will come to the opposite conclusion. People freely use credit cards to buy things over the Net; they send private e-mails trusting they will reach the right person and no one else; and they expect banks to keep their money safe for them. By and large, their behavior makes sense for them as individuals. Let's face it, consumers have other priorities. They don't take the trouble to check on Web sites' data practices, so why should the sites care? "Privacy," much as it is discussed, doesn't seem to confer a marketing advantage.

On the security side, meanwhile, company employees are careless with passwords, and their employers are careless with security overall. Insurance companies seem oblivious to the risks, and investors don't seem to care whether a company follows good information practices.

The threats don't seem real because it's in people's interest to keep them quiet. The organizations collecting data on individuals would rather the individuals didn't notice. The companies whose security is breached don't want to upset their customers, nor do they really want to let their insurance companies or investors know. And the people *breaching* the security, though they might like to brag, can't talk too much for risk of getting caught.

So you face a situation of blissful ignorance that may be shattered soon. There have been little eruptions already, especially in the United States. On-line and off-line, companies have been collecting data on individuals without notifying them. (Individuals can ask them to stop doing so, but the processes are cumbersome and there's no way for a consumer to be sure the data collector actually follows through.) The credit-card companies know too much; everyone is getting too much junk mail. And every banker knows a friend—not himself, mind you—whose bank has lost millions of dollars to clever crackers. More and more data is floating around, waiting to be nabbed . . .

Indeed, we may be on the brink of data disasters that only a little paranoia can avert. The attacks are coming from both sides: from people who want to undermine security on the one hand, and from companies and governments (including yours) who are collecting too much information on the other.

"Something must be done," say the authorities, because after all, security and privacy are a public issues. Now they will expect you to do it.

Unfortunately, right now, the wrong things are being done. Direct government regulation, as in Europe and probably soon in the United States, is generally the wrong tack. Aside from the threats to individual freedom of consumers and businesses to set their own terms, government regulation will always be a step behind the technology—whether it's companies' tactics in collecting and using data, or hackers' techniques in overcoming security barriers. Government regulation would give the appearance of solving the problems while allowing them to continue unchecked just as they do now.

But there is something you can do—not by direct regulation, but by using markets to do it for you, in a decentralized way. I suggest you ask the Congress and the Securities and Exchange Commission to require disclosure of security and data practices to investors and insurance companies, not just to consumers. Individuals may not be sufficiently motivated or compensated to consider privacy or security issues, but investors are. (Why that is the case is another matter, but those of us who hoped individuals would take advantage of their own market power to demand privacy have been sorely disappointed.) Once investors start to pay attention to the differences between companies with respect to privacy and security, those differences will start to matter.

The beauty of this approach is that it would work *with* the market rather than against it. Companies would compete to improve their security in innovative ways and to offer useful, intelligible ways of handling consumers' data. Meanwhile, it is possible to assess companies' privacy liabilities, and auditing firms stand ready to help them do so. It is only right that investors should be able to ask and find out this kind of information in assessing the companies they invest in. In the world of the Internet, there are a million ways to breach security . . . but the market can foster a million and one ways to protect it.

Use Markets as the First Defense for Privacy

On privacy, likewise, the solution is not to impose regulations, to eliminate the collection and use of data, and miss all the efficiencies and conveniences new technology affords. It's to put control of the data back where it belongs—in the hands of the individuals who generate it. By and large, that doesn't mean passing new laws, but rather setting new expectations—getting individuals to demand the terms and conditions they have a right to.

As president, you needn't pass laws, but rather make it clear to people how this should happen. It won't come about from a single set of laws or from the actions of a single sector of society. It will result from a variety of interacting forces and sectors. Your government needs to enforce statutes against fraud and misrepresentation, while private organizations such as TRUSTe and BBBOnline encourage companies to disclose their data policies—and enforce them if they are breached. Industry associations can encourage their members to behave better, and to promote data policies as a consumer benefit. For their part, consumers need to take the trouble to protect themselves, much as they lock their cars and secure their homes. Investors and insurers need to pay attention to the liabilities companies incur through unsafe or unsavory data practices, and to understand the benefits of trust for vendors who behave well.

This is not to say that your government should ignore the issue. Companies' data practices create a liability only where consumers' rights—to privacy and security—are recognized by law, even if the details are not specified. The increasingly activist Federal Trade Commission is saying clearly that one way or another individuals' control over their own data must be guaranteed. Meanwhile, the European Union has already issued a Privacy Directive.

Foster Disclosure of Identity and Credentials

Of course, an important part of security is knowing whom you're dealing with. And most individuals will want to know to whom they are giving their credit card, whose advice they are taking, whose news they are believing. Over the next few years, independent of action by government, a variety of private companies will offer "authentication" services, reputation services, identity certificates, and the like. You should encourage these services without requiring their use.

Yet even so, especially for the sake of people who live in other countries where the government is not so benign, you should . . .

Support the Right to Anonymity

. . . in the hope that anonymity will be cheap, safe, and rare (to coin a phrase!). Indeed, anonymity is an important possibility in a world where behavior is easier and easier to track. It is an important technical means for people to have freedom of speech where their governments prohibit it. (Anonymity is keeping your identity secret even as you do something in public; privacy means relying on someone else not to make public the details of what you do in private.) Anonymity may foster bad behavior and lies; it also fosters truth, from people who would otherwise be stifled by persecution—or simply by disapproval or censure. Crusading journalists, known for their discretion, may provide an outlet for giving credibility to anonymous sources.

Conclusion

All in all, Mr. President, the Internet should be the least of your problems if you can explain to the public why it will operate most smoothly and safely if you mostly leave it alone. Do support law enforcement, but you don't need a lot of new laws for the Net. Do support some consistency among states' tax regimes, but don't give the Net special tax benefits of its own.

Just let the markets work, with the small bits of guidance suggested above, and the news about you on the Internet is likely to be positive. Then you can deal with all your other challenges. Good luck!

SOLOMON D. TRUJILLO

Solomon D. Trujillo is former chairman, president, and chief executive officer of U S WEST, a leader in the telecommunications industry. Before becoming president and CEO in 1998, and chairman in 1999, Mr. Trujillo was president and CEO of U S WEST Communications Group and of U S WEST Marketing Resources. Mr. Trujillo holds a bachelor of arts degree and a master in business administration degree from the University of Wyoming.

U S WEST
1801 California Street Suite 5200
Denver, CO 80202

Solomon D. Trujillo
Chairman, President &
Chief Executive Officer

MEMORANDUM

TO: President-elect of the United States

FROM: Solomon D. Trujillo, Former Chairman, President,
           and Chief Executive Officer, U S WEST

SUBJECT: Managing Technology and People
           in Large Organizations

Congratulations on your election to office. The innovation,
prosperity, and potential we're experiencing at the dawn of
the twenty-first century make it a truly exciting time, with
huge opportunities for our country and for you as its leader.

As you know, opportunities often come disguised as challenges. To my mind, the biggest *administrative* challenges you
face over the next four years lie in two related areas:

1. making the most of new technology—specifically, the
   Internet and its e-commerce and e-business applications.
2. tapping into the potential of the people who work for the
   federal government.

Two Imperatives for the Information Age

The Information Age has just begun, and with it comes an
opportunity for both business and government to realize

unprecedented gains in productivity. Reaping those benefits depends on two imperatives.

The first is universal access—not just to computers, but to high-speed broadband services—so that we don't perpetuate a nation of digital "haves" and "have-nots." Improving access depends on eliminating the outdated regulations that restrict the growth of e-commerce and limit broadband access to large businesses and wealthy, densely populated areas.

> THERE NEEDS TO BE COOPERATION AMONG
> GOVERNMENT, BUSINESS, AND EDUCATION
> TO ENSURE THAT ALL CITIZENS—
> REGARDLESS OF RACE, LOCATION,
> OR ECONOMIC STATUS—HAVE THE
> INTELLECTUAL TOOLS TO SUCCEED IN
> THE NEW ECONOMY.

Removing restrictions on data traffic that impede competition and deployment of advanced services, and adequately funding the Universal Service Fund would make universal high-speed Internet access a reality. Bottom line—by letting the market work, our productivity as a nation will continue to skyrocket, as will our prospects for growth.

The second imperative is making sure education keeps pace with technology. There needs to be cooperation among government, business, and education to ensure that all citizens—

regardless of race, location, or economic status—have the intellectual tools to succeed in the new economy.

The United States has more than 300,000 high-tech jobs for which we can't find qualified candidates. We remain the world's undisputed technology leader, yet we've fallen behind other nations in a number of categories, including education and research spending as a percentage of total economic output. And we don't even make the top 10 list for percentage of 24-year-olds with a technical degree.

Given these two imperatives related to technology, I'd like to turn to some specific suggestions that I believe will prove valuable as you begin the task of managing the federal government.

Unleashing the Potential of E-Commerce. Stepping up e-commerce efforts is essential to the success of any large organization in the new economy. Doing things electronically can increase productivity while reducing costs, two things that were often mutually exclusive in the pre–e-commerce world. When Michael Dell revolutionized the computer industry by selling directly to the customer, he noted he was substituting "inventory with information." That comment pretty well sums up the speed, flexibility, and potential of an e-commerce world.

E-commerce can make transactions among government departments—and between government and its citizens—easier, faster, and less expensive. Today, the majority of government services are still delivered to citizens face-to-face. But depending on the type of service and the population using it, governments can save up to 70 percent by putting a service on-line.

And that doesn't include the time saved by both government employees and citizens.

At U S WEST, our customers can complete many transactions on-line, including viewing their bills, changing their service, and getting answers to commonly asked questions. We're constantly developing more ways to serve our customers on-line. It frees up our service representatives to tackle the more complicated issues, and gives our customers quicker, better service.

We're also using our Intranet to facilitate transactions between departments. For example, we have 11 different product catalogs, the result of a corporate structure of different business units that's not unlike the various agencies of the government. All these different catalogs mean redundancy and extra work for our people. So with the tools of e-commerce, we're building a "mega" catalog that contains everything in the 11 separate catalogs, and more.

Cutting across business-unit lines to have one catalog will mean greater speed to market, reduced operating costs, the flexibility to offer products and services of other companies as well as our own, and increased ability to change and expand product lines.

The benefits we're experiencing by moving to an electronic environment can easily transfer to the government. Federal, state, and local governments have already had success with things like on-line tax-filing support and renewal of licenses and permits. Going on-line means citizens can get the information and services they need quickly and easily. And the more accessible government is, the more democratic our nation can be.

E-commerce also provides new opportunities for sharing data. For government agencies, the faster and more accurately feedback is generated means the faster new programs can get into the system. Also, programs that aren't working can be removed more easily because of the greater flexibility of the entire system.

With all the benefits e-commerce brings at a time when everyone is struggling with reduced budgets and increased pressure to deliver better, faster results, why aren't all large organizations—including the federal government—doing the vast majority of their transactions electronically?

The main obstacle is a long-standing one: resistance to change. The transition to an e-commerce world means a fundamental change in how organizations do business. Embracing that kind of broad change is difficult—especially in the government, where agencies tend to operate as isolated "silos," unaccustomed to sharing systems or information.

Making the Transition to E-Commerce. Realizing the full potential of e-commerce depends on creating business services that can be used across agencies, but from a central platform that can be adjusted to the needs of each. That means finding a way to cut through department and agency walls.

Given this roadblock, what can you do to facilitate the transition to an electronic environment? The following five suggestions are based on our experience at U S WEST as we move to doing more and more of our internal and external transactions electronically.

1. Start at the top. Set concrete e-commerce–related objectives in terms of reducing costs and increasing efficiency. Clearly state what you expect in hard numbers, and also set the proper tone: become a champion for abandoning the silo mentality, for moving to an electronic environment that will allow departments to meet those numbers.

2. Invest in infrastructure. Going electronic doesn't mean destroying all your old systems and starting from scratch. Today's technology allows you to build on what you already have. With Y2K-related issues behind us, information-technology focus and resources can be shifted to e-commerce initiatives. That means investing in systems that allow the sharing of services across department lines—systems that can talk to each other, and that can connect federal departments with their state and local counterparts where appropriate.

3. Appoint the right people to key jobs. This might mean an e-commerce "czar" who acts as a high-level facilitator across agency and department lines. But even more important is filling key jobs with people who are progress oriented rather than excuse oriented—people who have a commitment to using e-commerce as a tool to accomplish the objectives you have set.

4. Insist on e-commerce in procurement. More and more businesses want to interact with the government the same way they do with their suppliers and customers—electronically. Across all industry sectors, more than one-third of companies have e-business operations in place, and that figure is closer to 50 percent in the transportation, banking, finance, and insurance industries.

Clearly it will become ever more critical to move to electronic procurement procedures for all purchases—large and small. For example, a unified platform with cross-referencing among the armed forces would mean consistency and cost saving in the procurement process at the Pentagon.

5. *Let e-commerce speak for itself.* E-commerce can be its own best promoter. As each agency sees how moving to an electronic environment can help it achieve the objectives you have set, they'll start to embrace the change. And that also goes for citizens, who will find their contacts with government to be far easier than in the days of endless paperwork and waiting in lines.

Getting the Best from the Most-Talented People

The shift to an e-economy means that the value of an organization no longer will be measured by counting physical or even financial assets. Instead, value in the new economy will be based on human capital—knowledge and creativity that can be shared with other people and organizations over the Internet.

This is true for government as well as for business, and it means that knowledge workers will continue to be in hyperdemand, in both the public and private sectors. It also means that smart companies—and smart governments—will devise new ways of viewing and treating employees.

Unlike traditional capital, human capital has the power to walk out the door. But smart organizations will keep their best people by creating work environments that nurture and grow human capital and promote effective collaboration.

Here are four things that any large organization, public or private, can do to attract and retain the best and brightest human talent.

1. Promote diversity. Minorities now constitute nearly 30 percent of the U.S. population, and that percentage will continue to grow. These numbers alone have transformed diversity from "nice to do" to "must do" as organizations scramble to find qualified workers and market to an increasingly diverse U.S. population. But if the numbers aren't enough to convince an organization of the value of fostering diversity, its benefits — a more dynamic, productive employee body more capable of responding to the needs of customers — surely will.

Those benefits start at the top. A recent survey by the American Management Association found that a mixture of genders, ethnic backgrounds, and ages in senior management teams consistently correlated to superior corporate performance. At U S WEST, 40 percent of our leadership and 25 percent of our board of directors are women, people of color, or both. We've found that the diverse ideas and opinions generated by a heterogeneous group like this is the best way to achieve exceptional results.

This also applies throughout the ranks. Today, companies — and governments — need people who are flexible, creative problem solvers and forward thinkers. You tend to get more of that with a diverse employee pool.

2. Reap the benefits of supplier diversity. The positive effects of diversity carry over to vendors, as well. By using a supplier base that mirrors your customer base, you can increase shareholder value, win and retain customers, and create jobs. With proper guidelines, supplier diversity can be a winning strategy for any large organization.

A successful supplier diversity program starts with making supplier diversity an integrated, up-front part of the procurement process, from supplier selection to managing supplier performance against commitments.

Procurement employees should have incentives—linked to pay or bonuses—to pursue diverse suppliers, and all major contracts should have an M/WBE subcontracting component. Finally, the bidding process must be competitive, with choice of supplier based on the quality of the company's products and services. For a supplier diversity program to be successful, the contractors chosen must be the most-qualified candidates in their field.

For any organization, commitment to diversity in all its facets should be an important business strategy. If we weren't committed to comprehensively promoting diversity at U S WEST, we'd have lost employees, market share, and revenue. For government, it could mean losing effectiveness, and the support of the people. In any case, diversity is a core business imperative, based on concrete organizational needs and the needs of customers.

3. Create an atmosphere that appeals to top talent. Businesses— especially those in the high-tech industry—are experiencing an unprecedented shortage of qualified workers. Finding and keeping top talent in a market where qualified candidates can choose from many opportunities goes beyond offering competitive compensation and benefits.

People want to work for a winning organization where their individuality is recognized and rewarded. The best organizations do that by creating an atmosphere that encourages people to do their best work. This includes formal and informal mentoring programs, flexible work schedules that allow employees to better meet the demands of both work and family, and resource groups that offer support, networking, and career advancement opportunities. It also includes a commitment to continuing education and training.

4. Promote continuous training and education. The most talented employees are constantly looking for ways to learn and grow. And indeed, lifelong learning can increase employees' communications skills, team participation, initiative, and risk taking. It also gives them more control over their own destiny, making them more marketable for better jobs.

Organizations can do a lot to contribute to that learning, thereby growing their human capital and giving the best employees incentive to stay. Although they may seem like corporate sacrifices or giveaways, tuition assistance programs, making sure an employee has the time to take an important class, management training programs, and company- and department-sponsored classes and seminars all help people progress in their careers and contribute more to their organizations.

Programs like these also give businesses a bigger source pool for filling critical technical jobs. Like many companies—

and like the U.S. government—U S WEST has hundreds of jobs going unfilled because we can't find candidates with the appropriate skills. Employee education programs help fill the gap, as do programs that bring the opportunity to learn skills like computer literacy to schools and communities.

It's terribly important as we move to an information-based economy to instill in *all* students from an early age the skills that will give them a wider career choice and alleviate the shortage of skilled workers. That means getting all schools—even the most remote—wired for high-speed Internet access and distance education.

The best education programs serve the needs of both the business world and the community. For example, U S WEST sponsors a program called Learning through Technology, which gives young American Indians in the Denver area and beyond the opportunity to gain specific computer and Internet skills they need to succeed in today's job market. The program matches the needs of business—for skilled workers—with the needs of a segment of the community that has a high unemployment rate.

With the Information Age upon us, successfully managing human capital and realizing the potential of technology can be the basis for a successful, smoothly running, dynamic government. I hope these ideas will prove useful in helping you accomplish this as you embark on forming and directing your administration.

I wish you all the best over the next four years.

LARS NYBERG

Lars Nyberg is chairman and chief executive officer of NCR Corporation. Before joining NCR in 1995, Mr. Nyberg was chairman and chief executive officer of Philips' Communications Systems Division. He also headed Philips' Data Systems Division. Mr. Nyberg holds a bachelor's degree in business administration from the University of Stockholm.

Lars Nyberg
Chairman & Chief Executive Officer

M E M O R A N D U M

TO: President-elect of the United States

FROM: Lars Nyberg, Chairman and Chief Executive
Officer, NCR Corporation

SUBJECT: Relationship Technologies: Managing in the
Networked World

You are about to take charge of one of the largest organizations in the world—the United States federal government. In your role as chief executive officer, you, and the executives you appoint, will be managing in what I like to call the Networked World. Managing in the Networked World will require your new appointees and the career civil service to think differently about both how you manage internally and how you relate to your customers, the citizens of the United States.

When we think of the Networked World, we often consider the evolution of computers and communications in the last few years—the laptop, the cellular phone, or the high-speed Internet connection to which we've all grown accustomed. But the Networked World consists of more than just these things. It is about everyone and everything being connected, and it is changing the way we live, work, and interrelate.

According to the Computer Systems Policy Project (CSPP), a public policy advocacy group composed of chief executive officers from America's leading information technology companies, the Networked World is a convergence of technologies forming an environment with certain life-changing attributes. There is little doubt the Networked World also will change the way government will operate in the future.

The projected growth of the Networked World is based on the Law of Network Effects, a simple premise stating that the value of a network increases exponentially when people or devices are added. For example, if someone had the only facsimile machine in the world, it would have no value. There would be no one to fax, and no one could receive a fax. With the addition of another facsimile machine, both suddenly have value. Now there is a network. Every time a single machine is added, the value of the network grows because of all of the combinations of transmissions possible.

In the Networked World, traditional barriers to productivity and interaction, such as time and distance, are eliminated. The network is perpetually "on," connecting people and devices seamlessly. And people can live and work where they choose without the negatives currently associated with telecommuting. In other words, they can be truly mobile without ever having to move.

These attributes suggest the Networked World is not about devices and bandwidth as much as it is about communication in a broader sense of the word. Communication as it relates to building relationships that will, ultimately, determine the value of the network.

Some may consider this to be a world of tomorrow, but it is taking shape very quickly *today*. In addition to the social, economic, and political implications of the Networked World, there are major implications for businesses and government, which must be able to compete effectively in this new environment. At NCR, we have aligned our business around delivering technology solutions for this new environment.

The Importance of Relationships

I want to introduce you to a new concept—one that is propelling NCR toward the future, and one that encapsulates where I think the next battle for competitive superiority will be fought within the context of the Networked World. The concept is Relationship Technology (RT). Though less familiar than Information Technology (IT), this concept, I predict, will become extremely important in all our lives. There is significant relevance, too, for how the federal government interacts with its customers, the citizens of the United States.

I want to share with you how NCR came to an understanding of RT; what we are doing to prepare our customers; and what we are doing inside NCR to prepare for a world in which Relationship Technologies are dominant.

Consider why Information Technology, by itself, is no longer able to meet the demands of the current business environment. The answer is that IT has failed to keep up with the need to learn from all the information collected. Over the past 50 years, IT has done little to support the relationships between companies and their customers. RT is IT with a purpose!

Sure, there have been some great advances in technology. Yet customers—in both the private and public sector—got fed up pretty quickly when automation came in and the personal touch vanished for the sake of efficiency. People dislike receiving computer-generated letters about late bill payments, a low bank balance, or an increase in their child's college tuition.

Are organizations missing something? Perhaps they do not yet have the right perspective on how networks are changing lives, and the world. Perhaps we all are too busy and too close to them to see their impact.

For many, network devices such as laptops and cellular phones are primarily tools to get things done faster and more efficiently. But for others, networks are changing things even more dramatically.

What Customers and Citizens Want

People are using networks to e-mail each other, to create their own Web sites, to download music, to shop on-line, and to assist in transactions. All of this access raises the bar of what people expect from companies with whom they do business. It also will increase what citizens will expect from their federal government.

And what do they expect? However you define your customers, they increasingly will expect a relationship. They want, and indeed demand, that businesses be in touch with them, respond to them, and anticipate their needs. What they expect is a relationship that has value to them. And they will reward businesses that provide this value with an old and sometimes forgotten response—loyalty.

Customer satisfaction has always required organizations to get two dimensions right: providing high-quality products that meet or beat the competition; and maintaining information systems that function 24x7.

However, the Networked World is creating a new customer expectation, indeed a new customer requirement. Those competing in the Networked World will need to excel in a third dimension in order to delight customers and to differentiate themselves from the competition. The ability to form relationships, and to nurture and grow them, is the third dimension that will differentiate outstanding organizations from those in the middle of the pack. Increasingly, these personal relationships are becoming tickets to the game, rather than the winning play.

And, yes, this third dimension—the ability to form relationships—will still be driven by technology. But this time the technologies will be designed specifically to build and enhance relationships with customers, not just to process their data.

Let's take retail banking as an example. Two of the most frequently encountered decisions in a bank branch are whether to waive a fee and whether to place a hold on funds. One of NCR's customers uses Relationship Technology solutions to understand information about its customers in order to deliver clear on-line directions, on a customer-by-customer basis, to its branch staff. Thus, customer representatives are advised in real time about waiving fees and giving immediate access to funds for the bank's most profitable customers.

Sounds simple, but this personal care has enormous impact on customer, and employee, satisfaction. It also requires the ongoing collection and interpretation of customer data, and the delivery of actionable information made possible by Relationship Technology solutions.

> THE CHALLENGE FACING YOUR NEW GOVERNMENT EXECUTIVES WILL BE TO DETERMINE WHICH AGENCIES CAN USE RELATIONSHIP TECHNOLOGIES TO DRAMATICALLY IMPROVE CUSTOMER SERVICE TO CITIZENS. AN INCREASED FOCUS ON RELATIONSHIPS WITH YOUR CUSTOMERS MIGHT VERY WELL RESULT IN AN INCREASE IN CITIZEN CONFIDENCE AND SATISFACTION WITH GOVERNMENT.

The bank I used as an example also is experimenting with other proactive services such as notifying its most profitable mortgage customers when rates have fallen below a certain level, thereby indicating it would be in the customer's best interest to refinance. Then, with the customer's permission, the bank will generate all the necessary paperwork. All the customer needs to do is show up at the closing.

These are examples of Relationship Technology solutions making a difference in bringing a business closer to its customers, and communicating more effectively to meet their needs. What business is this company in? Retail banking? Or is it more accurate to say this bank is in the relationship business?

I would encourage every business to do a quick mental check of how it would shape up in a head-to-head battle against a competitor with the intelligence and relationship management of the bank I have been using as an example. For the federal government, being empowered to offer customized service to citizens will be crucial, as citizens demand the same from businesses. The challenge facing your new government executives will be to determine which agencies can use Relationship Technologies to dramatically improve customer service to citizens. An increased focus on relationships with your customers might very well result in an increase in citizen confidence and satisfaction with government.

Many different kinds of businesses in this Networked World are using NCR's Relationship Technologies. In our own company, we are implementing Relationship Technology solutions enterprisewide. For example, the Worldwide Customer Services division uses our Teradata data warehouse to understand service volume and profitability on a daily basis by business unit, product, and customer. Raw data is turned into actionable knowledge, thereby increasing operational effectiveness, and ultimately our capability to serve customers better.

We are implementing Relationship Technology solutions because customers are demanding more. They expect organizations to know them, to know their needs, and to develop trusting relationships with them, while assuring their privacy is protected. It is always a two-way relationship these days, with the customer taking more control.

Businesses that have every process focused on this new brand of relationship management—across every channel, both physical and virtual—will build the strongest bonds with their customers. The result is powerful. The right offers reach the right customers, at the right time. It's a win-win for the business and for the customer. And it's the only way to compete and win in the future. Quite simply, relationships pay.

Where to Focus in Building Improved Relationships

In this new environment, where should companies focus their investments to really make a difference to customers? To get that third dimension right, let me share what I believe the three areas of focus should be.

Convenience. Convenience is the ability of people to access what they want, when they want. That's not as easy as just building channel upon channel. Today customers want different things at different times. Sometimes they want speed without the frills. At other times, they want genuine service and detailed advice. Organizations have to be prepared to respond to customers in different ways, on demand.

Value. There must be value for money and, in the case of government, value for tax dollars—the cost of products and services. We all recognize this as being very important. Cost is not everything, of course. But I think that in an age where businesses rightly spend so much time focusing on quality and customer service, they may overlook how much cost really does mean to many customers. There needs to be a sensible balance.

Relationships. This means the implementation of Relationship Technologies. In a world where many products and services are becoming commodities, and where they can be copied overnight, it will be the technologies businesses use to build relationships with their customers that will help them stand apart from the pack.

At NCR, we have adopted Relationship Technologies as the life force of everything we do in our business. By providing the Relationship Technology solutions businesses need to build relationships with their customers, we are building relationships with our own customers. This loyalty will not only improve our corporate performance, but also position us right at the heart of the Networked World. Relationship Technologies also can strengthen the position of the federal government and secure for you valuable relationships with the citizens of the United States.

EARNEST W. DEAVENPORT, JR.

Earnest W. Deavenport, Jr., became chairman and chief executive officer of Eastman Chemical Company in 1994, after leading the company's spin-off from Eastman Kodak. He joined Eastman in 1960 as a chemical engineer and became its president in 1989. Mr. Deavenport holds a bachelor's degree in chemical engineering from Mississippi State University and a master's degree in management from MIT.

EARNEST W. DEAVENPORT, JR.
Chairman and Chief Executive Officer

Eastman Chemical Company
P.O. Box 511
Kingsport, Tennessee 37662-5075
Phone: (423) 229-4085
Fax: (423) 229-1679

MEMORANDUM

TO: President-elect of the United States

FROM: Earnest W. Deavenport, Jr., Chairman and Chief Executive Officer, Eastman Chemical Company

SUBJECT: Leveraging Information Technology

A simple congratulations hardly seems enough at this most auspicious occasion, your election to the highest and most powerful office in the world. Achieving this honor at any time in history is certainly extraordinary and momentous, but never is that more true than now.

There is an old Chinese curse that says *may you live in interesting times.* And while the opportunities for growth and expansion seem boundless in our interesting times, they also bring with them a whole new set of issues and problems that have not fully revealed themselves. They are born of the ever-evolving digital age. How we meet those challenges—converting problems into prosperity—will be the hallmark of the current generation.

As a basic manufacturing company, Eastman may not instantly spring to mind when considering the subject of information technology. Certainly, it has been an education for us. It has been at times painful, but also very rewarding.

Responsible Care®
A Public Commitment

The chemical industry has suffered through extremely difficult times the past several years, more difficult than I have seen in my 40 years of experience. We have found it tremendously hard to increase margins on anything except those in short supply. We've lost pricing power and earnings, even when our very own country was enjoying its longest economic expansion in history. And we lost a lot of growth capacity.

> **IF AN OLD-LINE CHEMICAL COMPANY CAN LEVERAGE TECHNOLOGY, THE POTENTIAL FOR THE FEDERAL GOVERNMENT TO LEVERAGE TECHNOLOGY IS EQUALLY GREAT, IF NOT GREATER.**

Anyone following typical "bricks-and-mortar" companies would have noticed the urgency with which we reduced costs and the pervasiveness of our mergers and acquisitions. Unfortunately, these remedies weren't enough, and for the most part, they were only narrow solutions to a much broader problem. So how does a basic manufacturing company like ours survive in this digital age? It's simple. We move from a "bricks-and-mortar" company to a "clicks-and-mortar" company. If an old-line chemical company can leverage technology, the potential for the federal government to leverage technology is equally great, if not greater.

In actuality, the solution only *sounds* simple. In reality, our industry is experiencing nothing short of a revolution. While we are still on its cusp and just beginning to realize how it is shaping the world around us, it is obvious that technology is leading us into the twenty-first century. Although our business is basic manufacturing, we have realized that in order to succeed in this digital age, we must successfully learn how to leverage information technology. And because no business exists in a vacuum, we know that while it is important that we do this for the success of our company, we must also do this for the sake of all of our key stakeholders: customers, owners, suppliers, communities, and employees.

The benefits of leveraging information technology are basic, and also revolutionary. The speed at which business is being conducted is mind-boggling. By digitizing our infrastructure—which means more than just putting a dot-com after our name—we have built a *customer*-centric foundation that will shape our success. We must be able to give our customers what they want, when they want it, and how they want it. By providing a site on the World Wide Web, we allow our customers to directly order and track the products they want. We are able to reduce cycle time and labor, increasing efficiency while effectively responding to our customers' needs and demands.

We also provide the capability to interact computer to computer with our customers to manage inventories based on prearranged agreements. This eliminates the ordering process and reduces costs for both Eastman and our customers.

Leveraging Technology: Stockholders

Our *owners* win through leveraged technology. Information such as annual reports, up-to-date company news and business developments, investor relations information, stock price, and history is only a click away, thus giving our owners a clear overall business and historical picture of our company. One example of our interaction with our owners is made available by on-line proxy voting.

> THE BENEFITS OF LEVERAGING INFORMATION TECHNOLOGY ARE BASIC, BUT REVOLUTIONARY. THE SPEED AT WHICH BUSINESS IS BEING CONDUCTED IS MIND-BOGGLING. . . . WE MUST BE ABLE TO GIVE OUR CUSTOMERS WHAT THEY WANT, WHEN THEY WANT IT AND HOW THEY WANT IT.

An indirect benefit for our owners is the "Management Cockpit" that is available to senior management. This is an event-driven notification of company performance with drill-down capability on customers and products. Data is instant and more thorough, thus allowing for better decision making, which, of course, is always a benefit to the owner.

Leveraging Technology: Business-to-Business Solutions

As in any company, it is critical that we be able to receive quality goods and services from our *suppliers* in a timely and simplified manner. Technology has enabled us to provide Web-based procurement, which means that our employees now have on-line access to suppliers' catalogs, thus allowing direct ordering of materials. Billing processes have been simplified through the use of credit cards, allowing for cost reductions on both ends. Again, a win-win for both our supplier and us. I recommend that you ask your cabinet officers to see where their organizations can leverage technology to interact more efficiently with the federal government's suppliers.

Leveraging Technology: Communities, Customers, and Employees

Our *public* also benefits from the increased, advantaged use of technology. Through the use of our Web site—www.eastman .com—the communities in which we do business are able to find information that gives a clear picture of who we are. The unprecedented access our communities have to environmental and safety information is critical to reasonable, fact-based public-policy discussions.

Chemical companies have long been stereotyped as being dangerous and mysterious neighbors. By "virtually" allowing our communities through our doors, we are able to dispel these myths while showcasing how integral the industry is to an increasing standard and quality of living.

Technology is also helping all manufacturers be better corporate citizens by making way for monitoring processes that ensure compliance and more accurate record maintenance and regulatory reporting. Again, our public reaps these rewards as well.

Perhaps most important, leveraged technology has benefited our employees. Like many other companies, Eastman has aggressively searched for ways to be more competitive in the global arena. Part of that strategy means reducing both labor and nonlabor costs. Therefore, it became our challenge to find ways for us to do more with less. Again, technology was the key to finding the answer.

Beginning in 1996, a company Intranet was introduced to employees as a means to have quick and easy access to information and document sharing. More than that, it allowed for self-service.

Up-to-date, on-line directories shrink our 16,000-plus employees down to a single desktop. On-line training via the Intranet now allows employees to receive training from their work area, eliminating the need to schedule and plan to be away from the office. Business can now be conducted 24 hours a day, seven days a week, as information can be accessed at any time, from any location.

While productivity has increased, employees have also been given more direct control over their company benefits plans and options. Again, this information can be accessed around the clock. Employees can now handle personal business at their discretion and on their schedules. Transactions can be made in real time, on weekends, during holidays, and after hours. On-line investment services are also available to employees via the Internet allowing them to not only check their balance, but to manage their own investments.

We are exploring the use of the Internet and extranet as ways of communicating more effectively with our retirees, making our community even larger. We have also partnered with a local cable company to provide a channel dedicated to broadcasting 10 minutes of Eastman news items every two hours.

Through these means, we were able to discontinue our monthly newspaper, thus reducing costs and labor.

To summarize, leveraged information technology has allowed Eastman to reduce labor, better manage raw-material purchases, reduce nonlabor costs overall, reduce many of the time-consuming and expensive interactions with customers, provide an improved work environment, and establish a more effective means of communication. Simply put, information technology has allowed us to be better at what we do. I firmly believe that technology is the key to any business's success, and in many cases, it's the basis of the ability to survive in industry. I believe that to be true of our future government's success as well. We do indeed live in interesting times. But it isn't a curse, it's a blessing that provides us unlimited opportunities to do what this country does so well: prosper. It is my sincere hope that you are able to make the most of these times for yourself and for our country.

JAMES J. FORESE

James J. Forese is chairman and chief executive officer of IKON Office Solutions, a leading provider of technology solutions that helps businesses communicate. Mr. Forese came to IKON (formerly Alco Standard Corporation) in 1996. Prior to joining IKON, Mr. Forese spent 36 years at IBM Corporation in numerous executive positions. Mr. Forese holds a bachelor's degree in electrical engineering from Rensselear Polytechnic Institute and a master of business administration degree from MIT.

James J. Forese
Chairman and
Chief Executive Officer

70 Valley Stream Parkway
Malvern, PA 19355
Telephone 610 408 7269
Fax 610 725 8279

MEMORANDUM

TO: President-elect of the United States

FROM: James J. Forese, Chairman and Chief Executive
Officer, IKON Office Solutions

SUBJECT: A Five-Step Plan for Improving Organizations

The Challenge

The most recent annual report of the President's Council of
Economic Advisers (CEA) examines a great mystery: Why do
productivity benefits typically lag well behind the introduction
of major technological advances? Prominent MIT economics
professor Paul Krugman found the CEA's analysis of this phe-
nomenon so intriguing that he devoted an entire *New York
Times* column to it shortly after the CEA's report was issued.
In that piece, Krugman notes that "Digital faxes, video games
and the personal computer all date from the late 70's and early
80's . . . But until 1996 or so, there was simply no sign of a fundamental improvement in economic performance . . . And then,
suddenly, the fancy technology started to pay off. What took it
so long?"

Like the CEA, Krugman finds organizational inertia to be
the key to the puzzle, and he too notes that electrification didn't
deliver a big productivity benefit until after World War I,

though the light bulb was invented in 1879. "The problem," he writes, "was that simply replacing steam engines with electric motors didn't do much: businesses had to rethink the whole concept. Traditional factories were compact, multistory buildings—the optimal design when power had to be conveyed via shafts and belts from a steam engine in the basement. Only when manufacturers realized the advantages of a sprawling, one-story structure, each with a machine driven by its own motor—in particular, the benefits of having plenty of room to move people and materials around—did electrification really show what it could do. And this took decades. The parallel is clear. Putting a computer on every desk didn't do much by itself. Only by changing the whole organization of work could business really reap the rewards of the digital age."

Nevertheless, while there have been significant technology-driven efficiency gains in recent years, our national productivity gains are nowhere near what they should be in realizing the potential of the digital age. All too many organizations in both the private and public sectors remain mired in old, inefficient ways of conducting their operations.

Creating Solutions

I would suggest that the 14 departments and over 100 independent agencies and commissions of the federal government optimize the productivity benefits of new office technologies by adopting a variation of IBM's famous "Think" motto: *"Think Again."* I would like to share with you a five-step plan for improving organizations in both the public and private sectors. The idea is to take a good hard look at the assumptions that underlie current ways of operating. This means taking nothing for granted. Implementing the latest in networked digital technologies yields little if it simply automates obsolete or obsolescent processes. As Dr. Michael Hammer and James Champy note in *Reengineering the Corporation:* "The fundamental error that most companies commit when they look at technology is to view it through the lens of their existing processes. They ask, 'How can we use these new technological capabilities to enhance or streamline or improve what we are already doing?' Instead, they should be asking, 'How can we use technology to allow us to do things that we are *not* already doing?'"

PUTTING A COMPUTER ON EVERY DESK DIDN'T DO MUCH BY ITSELF. ONLY BY CHANGING THE WHOLE ORGANIZATION OF WORK COULD BUSINESS REALLY REAP THE REWARDS OF THE DIGITAL AGE.

Identifying processes that need to be revised, replaced, or simply eliminated requires examining, in a comprehensive way, how work flows throughout the organization. The key word there is "comprehensive." It is not cost-effective to approach systems upgrades in a gradual way, adding a new component here or there. While it is wise to try to leverage existing investments in information technology, it is imprudent to "let the tail wag the dog"—to fixate on maximizing the value of old hardware and software at the expense of creating a system that best meets the organization's communications needs going forward. Moreover, even if an entirely new array of office technology *is* cost-justified, the fresh start should not entail using one-size-fits-all solutions right off the shelf; it should be based on a careful appraisal of user-specific needs. In fact, users should be engaged as active partners during all phases of system design and implementation, since this engagement will give them a real sense of ownership in the final product—which is vital both to the system's proper operation and to organizational morale.

IDENTIFYING PROCESSES THAT NEED TO BE REVISED, REPLACED, OR SIMPLY ELIMINATED REQUIRES EXAMINING, IN A COMPREHENSIVE WAY, HOW WORK FLOWS THROUGHOUT THE ORGANIZATION. THE KEY WORD THERE IS "COMPREHENSIVE." IT IS NOT COST-EFFECTIVE TO APPROACH SYSTEMS UPGRADES IN A GRADUAL WAY, ADDING A NEW COMPONENT HERE OR THERE.

Of course, pursuing a comprehensive approach brings certain risks that must be managed carefully. Conducting a top-to-bottom assessment and overhaul of organizational processes can incur budget-crushing expense. Just as bad, the entire effort can fizzle on the launch pad as fact-finding becomes an end in itself, resulting in "analysis paralysis." These are problems to look out for.

At IKON, we have helped numerous clients guard against these risks by following a five-step plan for technology improvements. While we use it when looking at issues such as systems upgrades, I am convinced the general approach can be used when attempting to improve the overall health and performance of organizations. I suggest that your agency heads consider using this approach when assessing the state of their organizations and develop action steps to improve the agency.

- First, discovery. This step consists of conducting a needs analysis based on a questionnaire, in-depth interviews, and inspection of the technological capabilities, as well as other capabilities, that are already in place.

  This fact-finding is conducted in a very hands-on way. For example, it is critical for the engineers who are designing a new network to know precisely what real-world demands will be made on that system—just as an architect must visit a proposed building site before beginning design work in order to determine what kind of wind shear, topographical contours, traffic congestion, and other environmental factors must be addressed in the site design.

  When conducted by well-trained, experienced professionals using a standardized methodology, this process will yield a wealth of critical information without getting bogged down in excess detail. Again, the process of designing a building provides an apt comparison: In a preliminary on-site visit, the educated eye of an architect can quickly determine what geological issues must be dealt with without turning over every rock at the building site.

THE EASE OF PUTTING THE NEW SYSTEM IN PLACE IS DIRECTLY PROPORTIONAL TO THE CARE THAT GOES INTO THE EARLIER PHASES OF THE OVERALL EFFORT. ASSUMING THAT THE SYSTEM HAS BEEN WELL DESIGNED AND THE HARDWARE AND SOFTWARE WELL CHOSEN, THE FOCUS OF THE IMPLEMENTATION PHASE SHOULD BE ON ENSURING THAT ALL THE PIECES OF THE PUZZLE ARE BROUGHT TOGETHER IN A LOGICAL ORDER.

The discovery phase must develop a true fusion of perceptions between those who will design and those who will use the system. The system engineers and ultimate end-users must be entirely of one mind about the goals and capabilities of the new system. Built into this assessment process must be a "best of all worlds" mentality—that is, engineers and end users alike must not constrain themselves by the limitations of the current system, but must rather open themselves up to the possibilities presented by the removal of those limitations.

- Second, design. This phase involves the development of both an overall conceptual design for the system and actual blueprints that draw on input from various technical specialists—just as a building's blueprints reflect the collective knowledge of structural engineers, HVAC professionals, plumbing experts, and specialists in many other building trades. The best systems are those that are modular, allowing for "plug-and-play" flexibility and easy integration of new elements in the future. If different parts of an installed system prove incompatible with one another because of technical oversights during the design phase, it can be expensive to reconfigure components that are already in place.

- Third, plan. This is our term for the benchmark-testing phase of a new system. It can even involve creating a prototype of the proposed system in a laboratory environment and testing it in a way that mimics the demands that will ultimately be placed on the system. Making the test realistic depends above all upon conducting this exercise in cooperation with individuals who will actually be users of the system once installed.

- Fourth, implementation. The ease of putting the new system in place is directly proportional to the care that goes into the earlier phases of the overall effort. Assuming that the system has been well designed and the hardware and software well chosen, the focus of the implementation phase should be on ensuring that all the pieces of the puzzle are brought together in a logical order. If various components aren't available on site at the proper time, it can hold up the installation of other components, adding needlessly to the time and expense of the entire project.

- Fifth, support. System designers can't just head for the exit once the new system is up and running. They have to be on call to offer prompt assistance concerning both the technological side of the newly implemented office system and the business side—that is, how the system serves organizational goals.

To be a trusted source of support, system designers must be wholly candid in dealing with system users, and proper expectation setting is critical. Every new system has a beta-testing period where minor flaws are ironed out and users gain knowledge of how the solution operates under actual working conditions. Typically, this is a time when user nerves fray easily, and system designers should give users clear and ample warning that they can expect such a period of frustration. At the same time, users should be told that they can also expect whatever help they need to resolve these transitional issues in a timely manner.

Clearly, proper management of projects as large and complex as those the federal government faces in optimizing productivity through the application of technology is a topic too vast to be encompassed by any one memo. However, it is my hope that the points discussed here and the expertise that IKON offers clients can provide some useful guidance as your administration takes the reins and begins to evaluate the existing government processes and works to enhance the productivity of federal departments, agencies, and commissions with your guidance.

And as you know, there has never been a more auspicious time to do so. Recent gains in digital, networked, office technologies and the pervasiveness of the World Wide Web have made it possible to assemble, process, and transmit data with a degree of integration and speed that was inconceivable in the era of analog technology deployed on a stand-alone basis. The trade-off is that optimizing new technology requires *much more careful planning* than was needed in the analog age—when organizations seeking to increase their efficiency had to be concerned only with finding the best location for their new photocopier, not with determining the best design for their LAN or WAN, or the integration of distributed processes across the country, and even around the world.

Your team will face a real challenge in working with the federal bureaucracy to harness the tremendous power that today's systems can deliver and determining how best to implement those technologies so that the learning curve and trial-and-error period is shortened. But when you meet that challenge you will earn your administration an enduring place in the history books for closing the productivity gap.

RICHARD JOHNSON

Richard Johnson is founder, chairman, chief executive officer, and president of HotJobs.com, established in 1996 as the first truly interactive job board on the Internet. In 1988, he cofounded Otec, Inc., one of New York City's largest technical search firms. In 1995 he created New Media Labs, a research and development firm. Mr. Johnson holds a bachelor's degree from Bucknell University.

MEMORANDUM

TO: President-elect of the United States

FROM: Richard Johnson, Founder, Chairman, Chief
             Executive Officer, and President, HotJobs.com

SUBJECT: Technology and the New Economy

It is an honor to be given the opportunity to share with you
some of the things I have learned in today's fast-paced dot-com
world. I hope my observations will be helpful to both you and
your executive team.

Historians often define a social paradigm shift as a profound change resulting from many factors simultaneously con-
verging. Right now, we are at such a point. The "Information
Revolution" is causing more dramatic and far-reaching effects
on our society than it has seen since the Industrial Revolution.
Clearly, inventions like the printing press, telegraph, phone,
radio, and television have played a significant role in the country's technological and social advancements. However, the Internet marks the beginning of a new era. It is the Internet that will
change the fabric of not only our country, but also our world, in
ways only few can envision.

The Internet is the point at which mass media, personal
communication, and computer technology converge. Never

before has the world been so in touch. It has created a society in which within minutes of breaking news, the world knows about it—efficiently and affordably. People from across the globe can now share experiences together. Within minutes, organizations and individuals can research multiple sources, assess scores of information, and communicate their responses. Within minutes, grassroots movements can build the momentum they need to effect profound social change. It is clear that of the many social facets, which are being affected by the Internet, the most dramatic of all these effects will be upon the country's labor market. In building the Internet company HotJobs.com, I have gained a first-hand perspective from the front lines of the revolution, and I would like to share some of what I've seen with you.

The Internet, and its frictionless information flow, has shifted the balance of power in the employee/employer relationship in favor of the employee, for the first time in history. It has also shifted our economy from manufacturing to service based. Today, we have a more productive, technologically savvy workforce. In essence, the Internet has created an environment in which the knowledge worker has become the intellectual capital of the enterprise.

The Internet has also created a less loyal worker. Many argue this was inevitable. To be sure, companies only exacerbated the retention issue when many laid off thousands of workers in the recession of the late 1980s and early 1990s. Today, our economy is healthy and we are experiencing the lowest unemployment rate in 30 years. This is especially significant when you consider that in 2003, baby boomers will start retiring. Recently, the labor department stated that the labor market would have fewer people entering it than leaving it. In short, we are facing a shrinking labor force.

Let us consider the final catalyst: the proliferation of job sites on the Internet. HotJobs.com and other sites like it are offering opportunity seekers direct access to thousands, if not millions, of companies and jobs more quickly and more efficiently than ever before. The Internet has empowered people to seek positive change for their career with the click of a button.

IT IS CLEAR THAT OF THE MANY SOCIAL FACETS, WHICH ARE BEING AFFECTED BY THE INTERNET, THE MOST DRAMATIC OF ALL THESE EFFECTS WILL BE UPON THE COUNTRY'S LABOR MARKET. . . . THE INTERNET, AND ITS FRICTIONLESS INFORMATION FLOW, HAS SHIFTED THE BALANCE OF POWER IN THE EMPLOYEE/ EMPLOYER RELATIONSHIP IN FAVOR OF THE EMPLOYEE, FOR THE FIRST TIME IN HISTORY.

In the early days of the Internet, many suggested it was just a fad. The only fad-like aspect of the Web will be the ebb and flow of our responses to its cultural effect on us. For example, I am sure future generations will puzzle over the irrational exuberance exhibited by the stock market over the first few

Internet companies. As with other social realities (i.e., global warming), our temporal-minded society seems ill prepared to deal with long-term consequences. The issue of global warming involves many groups with varying interests and only future generations will see which group was in the right.

I strongly believe everyone should pay heed to the social issues in the world around them. Many have died so that we may have the right to vote, have an opinion, and speak our minds. Therefore, it is not simply our right to exercise these virtues, but it is our responsibility. Still, many remain silent about our current issues and personally, this is something I cannot understand.

Mr. President, I humbly realize I may be telling you things you already know. As president, you will be involved with and shape many of the day's issues. This truly is a great responsibility. I firmly believe that of all the issues you come across during your term, none may have more far-reaching social implications than the Internet.

It is important for the leadership of this country to understand the power of a networked society. The Internet provides the possibility of more effective health care systems, better access to information, and more efficient communication, and this should not be limited to the privileged members of our society. A "digital divide" would have as extreme negative consequences on individuals as on the country. We *must* provide everyone with the power of the Internet. It is becoming increasingly clear: The key to being and staying globally competitive is to provide the Internet, and all its possibilities, to all of our children. The government must take a responsible role by investing in the electronic infrastructure of our nation's school systems and getting all the nation's children on-line, early. This is no subsidy, this is a sound investment in the future of our children, and hence, in the future of the United States.

Clearly, issues such as the electronic readiness of our children and Internet policy will not be the only ones to cross your desk, but harnessing the power of the Internet is too much to be left to chance. The Internet has just begun to touch our lives. We must understand that we are facing a new chapter in our society where change is happening quicker than we can even realize. And like global warming, it may be quite some time before we fully assess the impact of these changes. Mr. President, I believe we can do better. With an understanding of the factors at work, you can leave a lasting impression on our economy, perhaps the global economy, as well as on every American and on our cultural institutions. Your legacy will be determined by how well you respond to the events of today, which are revolving around the one thing that has changed everything for us, the Internet. I believe history will prove it to be true: The Internet was, in fact, the single most important event of not only your presidency, but also of this century.

A ppendix

ARAMARK is a $7 billion world leader in providing managed services—food and support services, uniform and career apparel, and child-care and early-education programs. Headquartered in Philadelphia, ARAMARK has over 150,000 employees serving 15 million people at 500,000 locations in 15 countries every day. For the year 2000, ARAMARK ranked among the top 100 Most-Admired Companies by *Fortune* magazine and was ranked the third highest among all private companies in the report. Over the past 10 years, the company's strong financial performance has placed it number 5 in shareholder equity and number 42 in earnings per share growth among Fortune 500 companies. ARAMARK chairman and CEO Joseph Neubauer rates among the top five CEOs in the nation over the past 15 years with a 30 percent average rate of return.

For more information, visit <www.aramark.com>.

BD (Becton, Dickinson and Company) is a medical technology company that manufactures and sells a broad range of supplies, devices, and systems for use by health care professionals, medical-research institutions, industry, and the general public. The company has a 100-year foundation of quality, reliability, and commitment to its customers and business partners around the world. It is committed to bringing creative and innovative solutions to meet the demands of the future. BD has served health care workers, researchers, patients, consumers, and business associates around the world for more than a century. To meet the demands of the information age, BD is currently building Web sites for all its major locations and regions.

For more information, visit <www.bd.com>.

Conoco, Inc. is an integrated, international energy company with 16,700 worldwide employees, headquartered in Houston, Texas. The company had revenues of $27 billion in 1999 and operates in more than 40 countries. Conoco is celebrating its 125th anniversary in the year 2000. Its major business activities include exploration and production; refining, marketing, supply, and transportation; and power. In 1999 Conoco received two major, industrywide designations: top ranking among 14 of the world's largest oil companies by Schroder and Company for exploration and production performance during the past five years; and the premier position for European refiners by Wood MacKenzie, which measured 19 international oil companies' refining operations for net cash margin per barrel.

For more information, visit <www.conoco.com>.

EarthLink is the world's second-largest Internet service provider. Headquartered in Atlanta, Georgia, combined with seven other locations nationwide, EarthLink boasts a workforce of more than

5,500 and an annualized revenue of nearly $650 million. It focuses on providing access, information, assistance, and services to its members to encourage their introduction to the Internet and to provide them with a satisfying user experience. In March 2000, EarthLink unveiled its fee-based Web-hosting service, EarthLink Biz, focused on helping small businesses tap into the expansive sales, marketing, and communications opportunities available on the Internet.

For more information, visit <www.earthlink.com>.

Eastman Chemical Company is a leading international chemical company that produces more than 400 chemicals, fibers, and plastics. Eastman is the world's largest supplier of polyester plastics for packaging; a leading supplier of coatings raw materials, specialty chemicals, and plastics; and a major supplier of cellulose acetate fibers and basic chemicals. The company is one of the top 10 global suppliers of custom-manufactured fine chemicals for pharmaceuticals, agricultural chemicals, and other markets. Headquartered in Kingsport, Tennessee, Eastman manufactures and markets plastics, chemicals, and fibers. The company employs 15,000 people in more than 30 countries and had 1999 sales of $4.6 billion.

For more information, visit <www.eastman.com>.

EDventure Holdings, majority-owned by Esther Dyson, is managed by president and CEO Daphne Kis. It publishes *Release 1.0,* a monthly newsletter, and sponsors two annual conferences: PC (Platforms for Communication) Forum in the United States and EDventure's High Tech Forum in Europe. *Release 1.0* covers software, the Internet, e-commerce, convergence, on-line services, messaging, data networking, groupware, streaming media, enterprise applications, wireless communications, intellectual property, and other unpredictable topics. *Release 1.0* is widely quoted and known for its witty commentary and early insight into industry trends. EDventure's PC Forum is now in its 23rd year and routinely attracts more than 750 of the Internet/communications industry's leading players. EDventure's High Tech Forum brings together the key players in Europe's burgeoning Internet community.

For more information, visit <www.edventure.com>.

Eli Lilly and Company employs more than 31,000 people worldwide and market its medicines in 179 countries. Lilly is engaged in the discovery, development, manufacture, and sale of pharmaceutical products consisting of the following pharmaceutical groups: neurosciences, endocrinology, anti-infectives, cardiovascular, gastrointestinal, oncology, and animal health. It has major research and development facilities in 9 countries and conducts clinical trials in more than 30 countries.

For more information, visit <www.lilly.com>.

Gentiva Health Services is a leading provider of home health services in the United States and Canada. Through its network of approximately 400 locations, Gentiva employs a team of 70,000 caregivers and provides health services for over 425,000 patients and clients each year. Customers include managed-care organizations, employers, governmental agencies, hospitals, and individuals, who rely on Gentiva as their single source or a variety of home health services.

For more information, visit <www.gentiva.com>.

The Guardian Life Insurance Company of America, with nearly 6,000 employees and almost 2,400 financial representatives in 119 general agencies, is the fourth-largest mutual life insurance company in the United States. In the year 2000 list of Fortune 500 companies, Guardian was ranked 194. Founded in 1860, Guardian and its subsidiaries today provide almost three million people with life and disability income insurance, retirement services, and investment products such as mutual funds, securities, variable life insurance, and variable annuities. Guardian also supplies employee-benefits programs to 4.5 million participants, including life, health, and dental insurance, as well as qualified pension plans.

For more information, visit <www.theguardian.com>.

H. J. Heinz Company, with 5,700 varieties and 38,600 employees in 200 countries and territories, is one of the world's great food companies. The $9.2 billion company manufactures and markets processed-food products and the ingredients for food products throughout the world. Products include ketchup, sauces and condiments, pet food, tuna and other seafood products, baby food, frozen entrees, juices, and other processed foods.

For more information, visit <www.heinz.com>.

The Home Depot, founded in 1978 in Atlanta, Georgia, is the world's largest home-improvement retailer, with over 900 stores in the United States, Canada, Puerto Rico, and Chile. The Home Depot currently operates in 45 states in the United States, as well as in five Canadian provinces. In 1998 it opened stores in Chile and Puerto Rico. The Home Depot expects to be operating over 1,900 stores in the Americas by the end of 2003. Voted America's

Most-Admired Specialty Retailer by *Fortune* magazine for six straight years, The Home Depot aims to give consumers the lowest prices and the highest levels of customer service. The Home Depot stores cater to do-it-yourselfers, as well as home-improvement, construction, and building-maintenance professionals. Each store stocks approximately 40,000 to 50,000 different kinds of building, home improvement, and lawn and garden products. The newer stores include 15,000- to 25,000-square-foot garden centers.

For more information, visit <www.homedepot.com>.

HotJobs.com is a leading Internet-based recruiting solutions company that provides a direct exchange of information between job seekers and employers. Over 5,000 member employers subscribe to the HotJobs.com on-line employment exchange, <http://www.hotjobs.com>. HotJobs.com also provides employers with additional recruiting solutions, such as its proprietary Softshoe and Shoelace recruiting software, its WorkWorld career expos, and on-line advertising and consulting services. HotJobs.com recently signed an agreement to merge with Silicon Valley–based Resumix, Inc. Pending regulatory approvals, the merger will combine HotJobs.com's award-winning technology and Resumix's enhanced hiring management systems.

For more information, visit <www.hotjobs.com>.

Ikon Office Solutions is one of the world's leading providers of products and services that help businesses communicate. IKON provides customers with total business solutions for every office, production, and outsourcing need, including copiers and printers, color solutions, distributed printing, facilities management, imaging, and legal outsourcing solutions, as well as network design and consulting, application development, and technology training. With fiscal 1999 revenues of $5.5 billion, IKON has approximately 900 locations worldwide including the United States, Canada, Mexico, the United Kingdom, France, Germany, Ireland, and Denmark.

For more information, visit <www.ikon.com>.

Marriott International, Inc. is a leading worldwide hospitality company with over 2,000 operating units in the United States and 57 other countries and territories. Marriott Lodging operates and franchises hotels under the Marriott, Renaissance, Residence Inn, Courtyard, TownePlace Suites, Fairfield Inn, SpringHill Suites, and Ramada International brand names; develops and operates vacation ownership resorts under the Marriott, Ritz-Carlton, and Horizons brands; operates executive apartments and conference centers; and provides furnished corporate housing through its ExecuStay by Marriott division. Other Marriott businesses include senior living communities and services, wholesale food distribution, and procurement services. The company is headquartered in Washington, D.C., and has approximately 145,000 employees.

For more information, visit <www.marriott.com>.

NCR Corporation is a $6.2 billion leader in providing Relationship Technology™ solutions to customers worldwide in the retail, financial, communications, travel and transportation, and insurance markets. NCR's Relationship Technology solutions include privacy-enabled Teradata® warehouses and customer-relationship management (CRM) applications, store automation, and automated teller machines (ATMs). The company's business solutions are built on the foundation of its long-established industry knowledge and consulting expertise, value-adding software, global customer-support services, a complete line of consumable and media products, and leading-edge hardware technology. NCR employs 32,000 in 130 countries and is a component stock of the Standard & Poor's 500 Index.

For more information, visit <www.ncr.com>.

New York Life Insurance Company, a Fortune 100 company, is one of the largest insurance companies in the United States and the world. Founded in 1845 and headquartered in New York City, New York Life and its affiliates offer traditional life insurance, annuities, and long-term care. On the investment side, New York Life's affiliates provide institutional asset management and trust services and through a subsidiary, NYLIFE Distributors, Inc., provide an array of securities products and services such as institutional and retail mutual funds, including 401(k) products.

For more information, visit <www.newyorklife.com>.

Pharmacia Corporation, a new first-tier competitor in the global pharmaceutical industry, was created in April 2000. It is the result of a merger between Pharmacia & Upjohn and Monsanto Company and begins life as one of the world's fastest-growing pharmaceutical businesses. Pharmacia Corporation employs more than 60,000 people worldwide and has research, manufacturing, and administration and sales operations in more than 60 countries. The company has a strong portfolio of pharmaceutical products, a robust pipeline of new drugs in development, and invests more than $2 billion a year in pharmaceutical research and develpment activities.

For more information, visit <www.pnu.com>.

PricewaterhouseCoopers is the world's leading professional-services organization. Drawing on the knowledge and skills of 150,000 people in 150 countries, PricewaterhouseCoopers helps clients solve complex business problems and measurably enhance their ability to build value, manage risk, and improve performance. PricewaterhouseCoopers refers to the U.S. firm of PricewaterhouseCoopers LLP and other members of the world-wide PricewaterhouseCoopers organization.

For more information, visit <www.pwcglobal.com>.

United Parcel Service (UPS), a 92-year-old company, is the world's largest express carrier and package-delivery company and a leading global provider of specialized transportation and logistics services. The company was founded to provide private messenger and delivery services in the Seattle, Washington, area. It has since expanded its small regional parcel-delivery service into a global company. UPS delivers packages each business day for 1.8 million shipping customers to 6 million consignees.

For more information, visit <www.ups.com>.

U S WEST (now QWEST) is a broadband Internet communications company featuring data, video, and voice communications capabilities with digital subscriber line (DSL), wireless services, and local communications services in 14 states. It provides communications services to interexchange carriers and other communications entities and to businesses and consumers, and it constructs and installs fiber-optic communications systems for interexchange carriers and other communications entities. Headquartered in Denver, Colorado, Qwest has more than 71,000 employees worldwide.

For more information, visit <www.qwest.com>.

Varsity Group Inc. is a premier college marketing company that targets the 18- to 24-year-old demographic where they live—on the Internet and on campus. Varsity Group reaches students online through the highly trafficked VarsityBooks.com, the nation's most-visited and best-known Web site for reaching the college market. Its user database is a rich resource, allowing clients to effectively reach wired college students with messages that target them.

Off-line, Varsity Group Inc. captures collegiate attention through College Impact, a grassroots, student representative, marketing network. Its representatives are specially trained to reach students on a peer-to-peer basis.

For more information, visit <www.varsitybooks.com>.

Wellpoint Health Networks, with more than 10,000 employees, is one of the nation's largest publicly traded health care companies. It serves the health care needs of more than 7.5 million medical and over 31 million specialty members nationally through Blue Cross of California in California and UNICARE throughout other parts of the country. WellPoint offers a broad spectrum of quality network-based health products, including open-access PPO, POS, and hybrid products, and HMO and specialty products. Special products include pharmacy benefit management, dental, utilization management, vision, mental health, life and disability insurance, flexible spending accounts, COBRA administration, and Medicare supplements.

For more information, visit <www.wellpoint.com>.

Yellow Corporation is a holding company based in Overland Park, Kansas, with operating subsidiaries providing services for the national, regional, and international transportation of goods and materials. The corporation's largest subsidiary, Yellow Freight System, is one of the United States' premier brands in the marketplace for business-to-business transportation services, offering complete ground, air, ocean, and rail transportation throughout North America and overseas. The Yellow Regional Carrier Group includes Saia Motor Freight Line, providing overnight and second-day trucking service in 12 Southern states; Jevic Transportation, a multiregional less-than-truckload and truckload services carrier based in New Jersey; WestEx, providing overnight and second-day service in California and the Southwest; and Action Express, providing overnight and second-day service in the Pacific Northwest and Rocky Mountain region.

For more information, visit <www.yellowcorp.com>.